# Elevated

## Virgil Herring
## and
## Drew Maddux

*James-Laymond Publishing*

We rise by Elevating
others.

KEEP ELEVATING
OTHERS!

---

Printed in the United States of America.

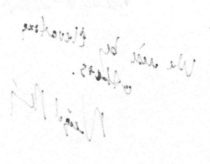

# Table of Contents

Perseverance ....................................................................1
Mindset .............................................................................7
Process .............................................................................13
Endurance .........................................................................21
Strength ............................................................................27
Speed.................................................................................31
Commitment ......................................................................35
Vision.................................................................................39
Creativity...........................................................................43
Love ...................................................................................47
Balance...............................................................................51
Analytics ............................................................................55
Coachability ......................................................................59
Competitiveness.................................................................63
Resiliency...........................................................................67
Grit .....................................................................................71
Adaptability.......................................................................75
Persistence.........................................................................81
Responsibility ...................................................................85
Vulnerability .....................................................................89
Focus..................................................................................93
The Process (Revisited) ....................................................97
Positivity ...........................................................................103
Confidence ........................................................................107
Embrace .............................................................................111
Passion ...............................................................................115
Enthusiasm.........................................................................121
Engaging ............................................................................125
Risk-Taker..........................................................................129
Grateful ..............................................................................135
Accountability....................................................................141
Transitioning .....................................................................145
Power .................................................................................149
Sport/Work IQ ...................................................................155
Grind ..................................................................................159

Fear ....................................................................163
Weakness ...........................................................167
Pain ...................................................................171
Failure ...............................................................175
Destiny ..............................................................179
Forgiveness ........................................................183
Loyalty ..............................................................189
Self-Control........................................................195
Poise..................................................................199
Happiness...........................................................203
Legacy................................................................207
Consistency........................................................211
Consequences......................................................215
Challenge ...........................................................219
Provoke ..............................................................223

# Chapter 1

# **Perseverance**

## **By Drew Maddux**

Perseverance is a tough one.

Perseverance is a word not used very much when describing someone or a group of people. When I hear the word perseverance, it is this certain quality that is hard to describe and very hard to articulate but, when you see it expressed, you fully know it and are very aware and encouraged by it.

Perseverance is the relentless pursuit, the embracing of a process, the getting up and trying to be better than I was last time, last shot, last meeting, or yesterday! It is a toughness but, it is so much more than that. Perseverance is conquering….perseverance is slaying that giant…perseverance is stepping into the arena and taking the shot even if you had failed over and over again.

Perseverance is very real to me. Perseverance is very close to me. Perseverance is defined by my daughter, Sarah James.

When I think about perseverance, I think about her and tears fill my eyes instantly because I think about her story intersecting with epilepsy and fully thinking she was going to die in a hospital room at Vanderbilt Children's Emergency Room on May 28, 2007.

Sarah James began to experience seizures as a toddler in 2007. She had 22 seizures between January and May of that year. Every seizure she had ever had lasted 3-5 minutes and we would call an ambulance, visit the ER, and rest and recover and come home that night.

She had been mis-diagnosed with the types of seizures and location of the seizures in her brain, so the many types of meds we were using to prevent them from happening were not working and caused much confusion among our doctors.

On this Memorial Day holiday on May 28, Sarah James had a seizure that morning in our living room. We called 911 as we had each of the 21 times before and the ambulance came and picked us up.

We got to the hospital expecting the day to be the same as it was before but, on this day something very different happened. Sarah James that afternoon broke into a second seizure for the first time ever and this was not a normal seizure like the others. This seizure lasted over 40 minutes and had the staff so worried as they tried to get it to stop, that over 8 -10 medical professionals were in our room attempting to care for this lifeless little girl.

I looked at my wife as tears streamed down her face as we both asked ourselves two pivotal questions: First, was Sarah James going to live?

Second, if she did survive, what would life be like for her? Would she be able to live a "normal" life?

Sarah James did survive that day and I am happy to say we found the best medical staff in the world for pediatric epilepsy and got her on meds that have to this day prevented any seizure activity.

She is a walking miracle as she is experiencing life and enjoying being a student. The reason I think about her when I hear the word perseverance is that every single day, we have no idea the difficulties she faces. She has learning difficulties, social unknowns, and other emotional trauma that haven't surfaced yet.

She wakes up and attacks the day and what is in front of her, striving to be better than the day before. She is an overcomer, she is a champion, she is uniquely and wonderfully made and displays perseverance to those who know her!

Learning and understanding are difficult but she chooses, with a great attitude, not to allow those things to keep her down. She chooses to rise again, embrace what is in front of her, and overcome the odds time after time after time.

Perseverance.

# Perseverance

## By Virgil Herring

The first thing that comes to mind when I think of perseverance happened May 2, 2010.

I stood on the deck of my house staring in shock at the most unbelievable scene I could have imagined. It had rained 23" in 48 hours. There was 7 feet of water standing in my home, the development where I lived was now an island that no one could leave, and I had just gotten a call that my business was wiped off the face of earth.

As I stood there, I had a destroyed home, no job and a tremendous amount of debt with no insurance coverage. I had a brief moment of pity standing there. Then for some reason, I made up my mind that I must change my mindset if I am going to get out of this predicament. My family was safe and healthy, my business was actually in my head, not some property, and I had a large database of clients that would still want to play the best golf they have ever played.

So I developed a business plan based around playing the game. Even though I didn't have my studio with all the technology, I still had high speed video on my phone. I set out on a mission to teach my players how to play using video of their swings in live action to better help them compete in 2010 and going forward.

I owe many thanks to Westhaven Golf Club for allowing me to teach there and all of my clients who rallied around me and my idea to help pull my family and I out of that debt and ultimately to a new home a year later.

There were so many bleak days, so much stress at home and all around us, and so much work. But at the end of the day, the moment I changed my attitude about how bad things were to how good they could be, it drove me to outlast the struggle that Mother Nature delivered to my doorstep.

# Chapter 2

# <u>Mindset</u>

## By Drew Maddux

I live by and teach to the truth that, "You are what you think you are!"

Mindset drives habits. Habits drive character development. Character development drives the paradigm in which you move and act.

There is no middle ground on mindset-simply, you either live from a positive mindset or a negative mindset.

In fact, in her book "Mindset" Carol Dweck discusses you either have a FIXED or a GROWTH Mindset! Meaning, you are choosing to learn, adapt, and live with positive enthusiasm or you choose to be a "know it all," be set in your thoughts and feelings, and live with negative energy.

Once again, no middle ground! It's an either/or proposition and we have the power to choose each day. Moment by moment. Decision by decision.

On September 11, 2001, 4 airplanes were hijacked by terrorists clearly focused on evil.

Two of those planes crashed into the Twin Towers in New York City that morning. One of the planes crashed in a field in Pennsylvania after one of the terrorists was maintained by a passenger on the plane and one of the planes crashed into the westside of the Pentagon in Washington D.C.

The natural instinct for those in the building was to run. Run as fast and as far as you can and get out of harm's way. BUT, on that day, there were heroes that did not run out but, ran back into the buildings to help those who needed it.

One of those heroes was Lt. Col. Ted Anderson and an account of his story was told this way:

"Anderson acted like a man possessed-as other people ran for their lives-he sprinted from his office toward the point of impact-spreading his jacket over shards of glass on a window seal. Anderson had another officer, Chris Bramen, boost him back into the building that was collapsing.

Together they carried two women out to safety-one woman was unconscious and the other woman badly burned.

Over the next hour, as the rest of the world anxiously looked on in shock, Ted Anderson returned to the blaze over and over and over again-at one point, he and Bramen were low-crawling through the infernos-screaming and yelling to be heard above the chaos and the roar.

Arlington County Firefighters finally restrained Lt. Col. Red Anderson and would not allow him to go back into the building-probably saving his life because just a few minutes later-the building collapsed.

Ted Anderson stayed at the Pentagon all day helping, serving, and saving people from danger. That night the building superintendent let him back into his office so he could get his keys to head home."

He drove home. He listened to 52 voice messages on his phone, took a shower, cried for over 30 minutes, and tried to go to sleep. But at 1:00AM his boss called and said "I can't sleep!" "Let's go to work!" "Put on your battle uniform!"

So, in the middle of the night, they headed back to the Pentagon because they knew our country was at war.

That is what soldiers do! That's who soldiers are! That is the mindset of a soldier!

Mindset is about being positive…facing your fears…serving others…and not thinking about yourself!

# Mindset

## By Virgil Herring

I will never forget the day in August, 2002. I was playing in a Pro-Scratch event in Nashville with Brandt Snedeker, leading by 6 shots after one round.

Brandt nearly missed our tee time the second day by literally 45 seconds.

I was a little frazzled by the possibility that we would be disqualified from the event if he didn't show up.

We both hit our tee shots well right on the first hole in the trees. As I get out of the cart to assess my shot, still steaming in anger, Brandt asks me what i planned on doing with my shot. "

"I don't know Sneddy, what are you going to do?" I offer.

"Here is what I am going to do….I am going to punch this 7 iron out in front of the green. Then I am  going to chip it in for birdie and we will roll these guys before this even starts," says the winner of 9 PGA Tour events.

Then to the bewilderment of my eyes, that is exactly what happened.

The team in second place had already hit 2 nice shots into the green.  I am sure they felt like they were going to gain at least one stroke on us, but Brandt had another idea. How about we just flip the momentum on them?

It occurred to me at that moment, that Brandt Snedeker had a different mindset than I, or anyone else I had ever taught. He had a very short memory for the negative outcomes, and an effusive belief that no matter how he was playing, that if he ever needed to hit a shot that could truly alter the outcome in his favor, that he would do it.

I had the honor to coach him for 8 years. I played in many events with him, and we never lost. His mindset was a "Rising Tide Raises all Boats" way of thinking. I always played better than my usual when playing with him. His belief in himself rubbed off on me every single time.

I had read it many times, from David Thompson, Michael Jordan, Larry Bird, and George Gervin - if I was going into the 4th quarter 3 out of 22, I would just keep on shooting because that just meant I was due to explode by going 10-10 in the 4th.

Well now I believed that actually was what and how the best thought. Brandt showed me that such a mindset was real, possible and A CHOICE!

I am so grateful for my time with Brandt. I tried to implement that attitude in everything I do. It has paid dividends for me multiple times in many different facets of my life.

What you think, you become.

# Chapter 3

# <u>Process</u>

## By Drew Maddux

"Trust the Process!" is something we have been saying for years to our players, parents, and coaches.

The process is what makes you.

The process will define you.

The process will prepare you.

The process should be the single focus.

Do not focus on the result or you will miss a step and if you miss a step in the process, you may have missed the very thing, experience, or lesson you needed the most.

In August,2011, we began our pre-season workouts to prepare for what would become a state championship season later on in March.

We knew we had a very good team and we knew we had great individual players. In fact, on this particular team, we had 11 of our Varsity players go on to play college basketball or football.

This team went on to win 37 games and did not lose a game in the state of Tennessee. We had great upperclassmen leadership lead by the TSSAA Mr. Basketball that year. We had a fantastic group of underclassmen that had bought into the concepts of being selfless and being others-focused.

We also had on that team one young man who was in 8th grade that went on to win a NCAA National Championship at the University of Virginia in 2019 and that is the focus of "Trust the process" I want to highlight.

In that very first pre-season conditioning workout, we were doing a series of tests to measure exactly where each guy was in certain areas.

Conditioning tests like a mile run, 4oo meter run, 100-meter dash, and a shuttle run.

Strength tests that would include bench press, squats, and a test of how many pull-ups each player could do.

This particular young man was in 8th grade but, he was already 6"6", very athletic, extremely skilled, and one of the best basketball players in his age group in the country. This was his first Varsity workout with the guys as we moved him up to play High school basketball even though he was an 8th grader.

He wanted to make a great impression and showed that he belonged…he wasn't just a Middle schooler but, he was here to play and be an important part of our team.

He did alright in all the tests, let's just say he was middle of the pack, but still very good for a 14-year-old competing against young men.

The last test was the pull-up test and he was the last young man to go. He jumped up on the pull-up bar, gripped the bar, pulled his knees into the air and proceeded to try with all his strength to pull his chin up and over that bar.

He tensed up, he growled, he grunted and never was able to pull his body up and we placed a 0 by his name.

This future NCAA champion, High school All-American, 2 time Mr. Basketball, 2 time state champion was not able to do ONE pull-up.

He was extremely embarrassed and felt a tremendous amount of shame in front of his teammates to the point that tears filled his eyes.

We broke it down and I asked him to my office because I knew we needed to do some damage repair to his emotions. We sat down in my office and the words that I shared with him were TRUST THE PROCESS, that he was being built for something that he could not imagine.

His entire career, which went on to be one of the most successful and prolific careers the state of Tennessee has ever seen, we continued to say to each other to trust the process, something amazing was just around the corner.

When doubt crept in when he was not playing as well, Trust the process!

When his shot was not going in at a high percentage, trust the process!

When that certain school was not recruiting him, Trust the Process!

When we lost a game or did not play well, Trust the process!

He bought into that concept and just continued to focus on the next right thing he could control.

His story is amazing because he even went to another college initially and it did not work out. So, he texted one day and said he was transferring and he was scared…I text back Trust the Process.

The Process started with an under-developed and scared 14 year old in the weight room on our campus where he couldn't do a pull up and 8 years later he stood on a ladder in Minneapolis and cut down the nets as a National Champion!

You never know what you are being built for but, one thing I am certain of, you must continue to Trust the Process as that next great blessing in your life is waiting for you as you take that next step!

# Process

## By Virgil Herring

The antidote for expectations.

It is easy to fall in love and glorify the amazing feats we watch on TV. Whether it be Tiger, LeBron, Federer, or Serena, many believe that is just what happens when you work hard. They set the expectation as taking down the superstar of today.

That is a recipe for disaster.

I am a huge believer in the process of being the very best you can be. I don't want to be Butch Harmon or David Leadbetter. I want to be the best version of myself.

My process is based around my very intense research of the greatest ever at many things. They all had similarities in their processes.

FOUNDATIONS:

- Integrity
- Honesty
- Responsibility
- Commitment
- Love
- Respect

Characteristics of Greatness:

- Hard work

- Desire to be a better version of me everyday

- Be a student...never stop learning

- Surround yourself with amazing people

- Give more than you take.

- Empathy for the grind and ability to smell the roses

Intangibles:

- Opportunistic

- Calculated risk taking

- Not be afraid to walk alone

- Lead those who will follow and follow those who are willing to lead you to your destiny.

- No one gets there by themselves.

To be the best golfer, you must follow a process that will deliver the best version of yourself every day.

You must hone your foundations of your swing, short game, putting, course management, mental management, emotional management and preparation for what you know and what you don't know.

Once you have a repeating movement that can propel the ball an appropriate distance to compete, all you are doing is aiming your shot variance to give you the highest chance of success over each shot.

Understanding the truth about what is the reality of a good shot from every place helps keep emotion out of our decision making. That is critical.

Playing the percentages all the time based around your strength and weakness profile allows you to game plan for optimization of your skills for the given moment.

If you execute your plan with reasonable precision, you couldn't do any better. Then I say you win.

The people who did that better than you allow you to learn, upgrade your talents, and set new visuals for your next best attempt at bettering yourself.

The process to your best golf, best life, best whatever are remarkably close to the same.

Due diligence to task, optimize strengths, set the plan, allow for adaptability, commit to each moment, and then give a proper self-analysis at a certain stopping point to start the process over again.

When your only expectation is process efficiency, you bring the best version of yourself that day each and every day.

What else can anyone else, including yourself, ask for?

Trust your process.

## Chapter 4

# <u>Endurance</u>

## By Drew Maddux

The great ones can last!

The great ones can finish!

The great ones can rise up!

The great ones are unwavering in times of mental, emotional, and physical exhaustion.

Endurance is a separating factor between the great and the average!

I was encouraged by a special young man his senior year in December of 2011. This young man is tough. This young man wanted to compete and win in every single thing that he did.

It could be a simple sprint or it could be a competitive segment in practice or a huge game against our biggest rival. It did not matter what the activity was, he was a relentless competitor that had the ability to push through and finish!

Classroom? Over a 4.0 GPA!

He served and worked in his church and community continuously!

He went on to be the first player in my understanding to win a state championship, be named MVP of the state tournament, and then named Mr. Basketball on the final day after we won our first gold ball!

He signed a college scholarship to Belmont University after tearing his PCL in his knee his junior year. When I say this young man had a toughness unparalleled to his peers, that was the truth!

But, on this night in a major Christmas basketball tournament against an amazing opponent, he even displayed a whole other level of what great endurance and toughness looks like!

We played in the Final 8 of a nationally recognized Christmas tournament against a prep school from Germany.

This team had double digit college basketball players, many now in professional leagues across the world. Their front line consisted of great size anchored by a center over 7'0. At the time we played them, they were one of the Top 5 high school teams in the world. They were good, very good!

Our starting PG had a sprained ankle and could not play this particular game so, at best, we had a very small percentage of being able to win.

We shifted some players around and downloaded a game plan to our guys we felt could give us a chance, but much of our success would hinge on the ability of this special young man to play maybe the best game of his career because of what we were going to ask him to do in handling the ball at the PG spot.

Before the game, I told him he was not coming out of the game so do not look at the bench. He was going to have to play the full 32 minutes from tip to buzzer and not only that, literally, handle the ball and be asked to make all the plays for us.

The game was an incredible game played in an amazing environment with over 7,000 fans in attendance jammed into the arena on a cold December night. We made plays, they made plays. We made shots, they made shots with this young man front and center in making play after play after play.

He was incredible. He made acrobatic shots. Made 3-point shots. Drove and got fouled, knocked to floor and would get up make his free throws. He grabbed rebounds. He dove for loose balls and accounted for most every point we had, either through scoring or assisting someone else.

It was the most brilliant performance I have seen in high school basketball. Late in the 4th quarter with the game tied, he dove for a loose ball at mid court and went over the press table. He was out of sight for a couple minutes and when play stopped, the officials told me I could sprint over and check on him.

I got to him and knelt down and he was agonizing in pain, holding his shoulder as he told me, "My shoulder is out of place."

We got the trainers over to him and they popped it back into place.

We were thankful it was his non-shooting arm.

This young man finished the 4th quarter on one arm and made a shot to send the game to overtime.

We continued to battle and play and won the game in double OT. It was probably the best victory our program has ever had. This young man fought through fatigue and pain and displayed incredible endurance.

He finished with 40 points and a triple double, finishing the game with only one arm.

# Endurance

## By Virgil Herring

The ability to outlast, outwork, and overcome the most.

Endurance is a physical practice that feeds the mind.

Endurance can be trained in many ways. Through pure physical training and running. It can be done doing games that are more difficult than the event you play.

The fundamental is to learn that you ALMOST have no limits to your physical endurance. The further you push, the further you see that you can go.

As soon as the mental habit of seeing no obstacle too big, no struggle too difficult, no pain too much, we create an incredible cycle of mental and physical endurance that feed each other. We do it until we have created a person who thrives on the work, the struggle, and the impossible goal.

This cycle is what I call the champions mind. The more I train, the mentally tougher I become. The mentally tougher I become, the harder I can train.

It all starts in the mind. It manifests itself in the body. It's a warrior mindset. They want it difficult, really difficult because not many people live like this.

The high road does not have much traffic. Exit the mainstream and get in the expressway to excellence.

# Chapter 5

# <u>Strength</u>

## By Drew Maddux

Strength is usually an attribute people speak to as it relates to the physical realm. When one thinks of strength, you image someone lifting weights, a mover carrying furniture, or even a big lineman blocking for a running back on the football field.

Sometimes you think strength relates to someone displaying dominance over someone or being the "alpha" in a situation or position of leadership.

When I hear the word strength, I think of my grandfather, James Edward Maddux. Granddaddy, as I called him, was a big man. He was about 6'4" and probably my entire life weighed over 300 pounds.

He played football and basketball at Vanderbilt University and served in the war in his lifetime. When he returned home, he used his genius to help start a structural engineering firm.

He possibly was the smartest person I have ever met in my lifetime. He was strong, detailed, articulate, and brilliant in all matters.

He was a leader and CEO and founder of an organization that had many employees. When I think of Granddaddy, I think of strength because I think of his humility, slow to speak and quick to listen, gentleness and approachability.

He had a way with people that made you become the best version of yourself. Many times, I would sit in his lap at his architect table or in his wood making shop and he would share lessons like "If it is not true, honoring, or encouraging, do not say it!" with me.

He had a way with people and I never saw him grow frustrated and I do not remember a day where he raised his voice or displayed anger.

He was strong because he laid down his own need to be right.

He was strong because he was always thinking of service.

He was strong because of his humility.

He was strong because of the way he loved!

# Strength

## By Virgil Herring

Strength comes from every facet of our being.

Obviously the easiest to see is the physical strength.

Maximizing your physical strength is imperative to your performance, no matter what you do.

Mental strength is what keeps you going when you think you have nothing left.

Pushing through mental barriers is an acquired talent. Emotional strength is a sign of control.

When we allow emotions to dictate our decision making, usually bad things happen. The ability to FEEL the emotion, allow it to BE, and then push past it with process is what separates good from great.

It is easy to notice when you are around someone of complete strength. They move the room.

# Chapter 6

# **Speed**

## By Drew Maddux

"Speed kills!"

Speed has become a major factor in the evaluation of athletes, teams, and corporations. Think about the NFL combine and the way a player can post a great 40 yard sprint time and his stock will skyrocket.

Or Tom Brady and his ability to navigate and lead a drive down the football field in the last 2 minutes of a game running a flawless 2-minute drill.

Lastly, Apple, Nike, or other Fortune 500 successful organizations that can go from idea to production to distribution to market availability seamlessly.

The successful entities work, live, and play faster and I believe have a sense of urgency to live or work each day like it is their last.

Life moves at such a fast pace and days, years, and seasons will be over in the blink of an eye.

Enjoy the day and have a sense of urgency.

The way we all should approach each day is like a 2 minute drill, never taking anything for granted!

Speed focuses on the connection between moments. The focus we should have is to win each moment, each experience, each day!

That means each and everything we do is connected to each other, leading to a comprehensive result.

Speed takes each moment, processes very quickly what just occurred, and is the connector to a response to win the next moment.

Greatness is impossible without speed. Speed is the conduit and bridge of moment connectors.

# Speed

## By Virgil Herring

Speed is the number one indicator of talent.

Whether it be in processing information, getting from one side of the field/court to the other, your fastball, or your swing….speed is king.

I train for speed first, like max it out speed. Jack Nicklaus said it best, "Swing as fast you can and then learn to control it."

We are seeing that today in golf more than ever. Clubbed speeds nearing 140mph and producing a playable ball flight.

On the court I envision the true speed of LeBron during the playoffs running down someone from behind.

He covered ground like no one else. Whether in the classroom, on the field of play, or in the office, it is wise to practice speed training.

Learn from your mistakes at high speeds. because under duress, time is speeding up in your head. If you learn your traits under fire, you will not only be more prepared for day to day, but really separate yourself under the gun.

Training for speed in decision making is also paramount in superior performance. The person who can learn to process information the fastest, make the best decision the fastest, and do it faster than anyone else holds the gold.

Speed….speed…speed.

## Chapter 7

# **Commitment**

## **By Drew Maddux**

Commitment is very different than just being a part of something or being interested in an activity, a group, a cause, or a relationship.

Commitment is the driving force that moves you, motivates you, and inspires you to be the very best you can be.

Commitment drives you to love, serve, and encourage another human being - that being your spouse, teammate, or family member.

Commitment also is what makes you come to life as you are accountable to a cause or something greater than yourself.

One of the elements of CPA Basketball, where I serve as Head Coach, is we love early morning workouts at 6:00AM.

We believe we coach each young person we are blessed to coach for who they are becoming, not just for who they are today.

The demographic I serve is 14-19 year old boys trying to navigate through the difficulties of the culture and the world and I believe is the most difficult group of people to try to mobilize as a group and get them to understand that they exist to be in relationship and to be a part of something greater.

Commitment is the attribute that moves them. Therefore, one way we teach the principle of commitment is to make them get up early in the morning on many days to be at the gym for early morning workouts.

It is uncommon to get up on a June hot day at 5:00am to be at the gym for basketball practice at 6:00Am. Think about it, the traditional basketball season exists in the winter and here are over 30 young men who wake up most mornings in the summer while it's still dark outside to attend practice 6 months ahead of their season.

Why would a teenager do this? What motivates them to swim upstream against the typical culture participator and jump out of bed and get to the gym before the sun comes up? Commitment. Commitment is what moves them, keeps them accountable, allows them to think of others before themselves, and to play to their strengths and allow those to be leveraged for the good of someone else.

Commitment is being taught every day. Yes, it helps make our program successful, but more than that, we are teaching and coaching for the men they are becoming.

So, when the alarm goes off, you wake up and go to work. When your son or daughter cries out on the baby monitor at 3:00am, you tell your wife, I got this one, you go back to sleep.

Lastly, when the culture tries to pull you or convince you to be something that you know is not right, you do the next right thing because of commitment!

# Commitment

## By Virgil Herring

Commitment in golf is pure decisiveness.

It is better to commit to something less than perfect than to not be committed to the perfect decision.

What is interesting about commitment in golf or another game versus human relationships is that we take our human relationships at face value way more seriously than the game, but we are way more committed to accepting our flaws in the game.

Not many would find it okay to commit to meeting our best friend or spouse somewhere, then decide to do something else instead and not let them know.

I see this happen in golf way to frequently. We know what we should do, we walk into the shot thinking correctly, but when we get ready to swing there is this devil on our shoulder telling us to aim at the flag instead of the middle of the green.

Commitment is/should be an all-in thing. Usually what is best for the team is best for you.

In golf I hear from my team that it is still an individual game. But I ask them all the time, "What decision are you talking about that I am asking you to change that hurts you to benefit us?" Of course, I never get a good answer because there isn't one. Whether it be for business, family, team, etc., what is best for the whole is best for you. Every time I make a decision, I think about how this could impact any of my relationships.

Foundations or pillars of your life require commitments. Without them, nothing can stand up to a little bit of resistance, let alone a storm of resistance.

Find your foundations and lay down your commitments. Pour concrete around your foundation, not sand. Learn the difference between foundations and paintings.

## Chapter 8

# Vision

## By Drew Maddux

"What you see is what you will become."

This is a thought and belief that I have lived my life for as long as I can remember. Nothing can ever be accomplished without first a thought or a vision of actually seeing the accomplishment first.

Let me put it another way, Draymond Green, forward for the Golden State Warriors, just spoke to this thought and said if he did not see himself as the best at what he does, he had already failed. He even asked the reporter that asked the question if he saw himself as the best reporter in the world. Draymond challenged the reporter and said if he did not operate from that Vision, the reporter had already failed.

Vision is the driving force that provides hope and hope is what is needed to rise up above your current circumstance.

I ask people all the time, "Do you live in vision or circumstance?"

Vision will keep you positive.

Vision will give you energy.

Vision will provide hope.

Vision will keep telling you that you have what it takes, keep on going!

When I was 5 years old, I drew a picture on a sheet of paper of a player wearing a Vanderbilt University basketball jersey and shooting a basket in Memorial Gym.

The picture was of myself in that uniform playing in that iconic place. At that young age, I already had established a vision of something that had been placed in my heart.

Every day through my elementary years and into my middle school years and then into high school, I woke up and saw that picture and did everything I could possibly do that particular day to make sure my actions, habits, and character was in alignment with that vision.

As I got to Middle School, I was already shooting 1,000 shots a day. I had workouts that would last hours upon hours while my friends were at the pool.

Many of my summer vacations were spent in gymnasiums around the country. I missed high school dances because of basketball tournaments and I made sacrifices none of my friends understood. But I had a vision and I was passionate about walking into the reality of that vision coming true.

That vision of playing basketball at Vanderbilt woke me up early. Made me study for tests when I did not want to and get up and condition in the dead heat of summer when I did not want to. That vision kept me accountable and was a check in my spirit in my decision making when my friends were doing things they knew they should not do.

Vision is power and I am thankful I was given that picture of me one day playing at my favorite university a sport that was my very favorite thing to do.

In November of 1994 as a freshman, I took the floor of Memorial Gym for the very first time wearing #45 (my Dad's number) for the Vanderbilt Commodores.

My mom brought that picture to the gym that night and reminded me as an 18 year old college freshmen that the vision I had as a 5 year old that had been on my mirror in my bedroom was now no longer a vision, it was real life!

Vision trumps circumstance. Vision will give you hope when you desperately need it!

# Vision

## By Virgil Herring

At its truest core, vision and the quality of vision is a true separator in the athletic world.

I remember playing with Brandt Snedeker many times where he read all of my putts. Many times he was able to see breaks that I could not.

SportsSense is a company that can show how good or bad your vision is, but I am sure the best hitters, shooters, wide receivers, and tennis players would measure off the chart with vision.

Vision can also imply a "6th sense" of where people are on the field, ice, or court. Gretzky was widely touted as other worldly in his ability to "know" where his teammates were going to be before they got there.

One is concrete and the other abstract, but vision is essential in visualizing success, seeing what is required to win, and seeing what needs to be done differently or better in the post event self-analysis.

# Chapter 9

# <u>Creativity</u>

## By Drew Maddux

The great ones are a little bit different. Greatness requires the uniqueness to see, think, and feel differently than those around you.

Creativity is in alignment with people who get a vision to set out to do something that will change the world. The first thing we learn about God is that he created. "In the beginning, God created the heavens and the earth." (Genesis 1:1)

And, because we were created in His image, we have all been extended elements of creativity. Being creative does not necessarily mean I have to paint, draw, or sculpt.

Creative could be the way you see situations, being a solutions provider, or even thinking of another way. The one thing that being creative does require is being positive. You must think you have something to contribute to make others or the world better or your creative switch will stay in the off position.

Everyone has unique abilities and have specific strengths that need to extended to all humans to make the world better.

I think about Steve Jobs sitting at his desk and thinking of communication systems to make the world better.

I think about the Wright brothers sitting on that beach and thinking about a machine that could possibly fly through the clouds to allow people to travel much more efficiently.

Think about Paul McCartney sitting in a recording studio with his 3 best friends and having a yellow legal pad and pencil in his hand and scribbling out the words to another iconic hit.

Or Phil Knight, sitting in his home office in Oregon and thinking there has to be a way to create a shoe for the athlete - and there is an athlete in all of us.

Mark Zuckerberg creating a media application to allow friends and family to stay connected regardless of distance.

I could go on and on and on and tell more thorough details to each of these stories and the genius behind their creativity.

We all share common attributes with all of these people in that the world needs us to be creative in our own special and unique way.

The world is counting on you to think about your giftings and areas you are passionate about and to figure out creative solutions to make it better.

Being creative is caring about others and thinking of others before myself and being a solutions provider, a gamechanger, and a world shaper!

# Creativity

## By Virgil Herring

When I think of creativity, I think of Seve Ballesteros and Tiger Woods.

Their ability to create something out of nothing was nothing short of miraculous.

Creativity is higher-level thinking that accesses the right side of the brain. An endless portal of vision and artistry. To be creative is such a special talent.

To be able to solve issues from an out-of-the-box manner is what innovates every profession.

Tiger's insane ability to create taught many of his current competitors today that what they were witnessing could be replicated. Michael Jordan did the same.

Being able to access the correct part of the brain is trainable and truly what the elite are doing daily.

# Chapter 10

# Love

## By Drew Maddux

To make a difference in this world, LOVE is essential.

Love is the most powerful force in the universe and is direct opposition to hate, but to love is to consider others better. To love is to stop comparing and competing with the guy next to you and celebrate. Celebrate even more for what they are doing than you would for yourself.

Love drives. Love moves. Love motivates. Love creates an environment and culture that is life-giving.

Love changes communities. Love changes everything and everyone. Love breaks down walls. Love creates bridges to the souls of others. Love connects you to a great calling and purpose.

Love conquers all. Love flows from the heart and we are a part of a culture that is losing its mind because it has lost its heart.

To make a difference, love has to be present! And our higher calling and purpose should be to leave places and people better and the only way that can happen is to love!

To make a difference, love has to be present! Love can create change, but Love is a matter of the heart and for it to be present, we must love from knowing what to do in our mind to allow your heart to lead and be the force behind all motivation.

One hero of mine taught me what love in action looks like when I was younger and really began to manifest in my college years. My grandfather, Billy Ramsey Cline, was diagnosed with cancer in his throat in 1995, my freshman year at Vanderbilt.

I loved playing at Vanderbilt for many reasons: Being in Nashville, where I grew up, being a third generation Commodore, playing in the Southeastern Conference, and building new lifelong friendships with teammates and coaches. But one of, if not the main reason, was because of the way it connected my family in closer relationship.

My grandfather was dying. He loved to watch me play and endured countless surgeries, numerous cycles of chemotherapy and radiation, and even had his voice box surgically removed. But with all those difficulties, he never missed a game at home or on the road. I heard many stories of him leaving the doctor's office after receiving a round of chemotherapy and jumping in the car with a bucket in his lap for the ride in case he got sick. That's love!

On particular day in Memphis I will never forget the power of love. In March of 1997, my junior year, in SEC tournament, we were playing Mississippi State. This was a must win game for us as we were sitting on the NCAA tournament bubble and needed one more win to secure a bid into March Madness.

With 11:58 in the 2nd half, we headed to a media timeout down by double figures and really not playing well. I was really struggling as well as I could not find my shot and only had 2 points and was extremely frustrated. As we headed to the bench, I looked up in the crowd of over 20,000 people and somehow found my Grandfather and made eye contact with him as he mumbled with his mouth, Come on Drew!

That was the shot of encouragement I needed. That quick glance and eye contact re-centered me and because of his love for me and being present even in the midst of his circumstances, changed me.

From that point on in the game, I scored 22 points, hitting a shot to send the game in overtime at the buzzer and we won by 6 points. As a result of this win, one week later, we secured our bid to the NCAA tournament.

My grandfather showed me what true love was. Always considering others better than himself. It was a selfless love that was on full display during his battle of that dreadful disease.

We are all here for a purpose, there are no accidents. Everyone has a special gift and special call, but in order to walk into the presence of those things, you must start with one simple reminder - love the next person in from of you the best way you can and watch the boomerang blessing that comes back into your own life.

# Love

## By Virgil Herring

Love is where it all originates. Life is love.

When we engage in something that entices our mind, spirit, and soul, and then have an all-encompassing moment where we are completely whole and present in that space, that is when love is formed.

Whether it be another human being, a game, or an occupation, you can like a lot of things, but when you are locked down and fully connected to the other with all of your senses glued into the moment and you receive that electricity from the dopamine high.....HELLO LOVE!

Once you find love, true love, it becomes the wind in your sails, the fuel for your motivation engine.

Let love ignite your heart and soul and watch your life soar to unforeseen places.

# Chapter 11

# <u>Balance</u>

## By Drew Maddux

Balance is a quality that is essential to greatness.

Balance is another one of those ingredients that separates average from good and good from great.

Balance is the description to living a comprehensive win-win-win life.

The people that are great that I have studied over years do not have compartmental greatness. Greatness flows into all realms of their lives - work, home, and citizenship (essentially loving people, places, things, and life).

If you achieve greatness at work, but have horrible relationships with your children or spouse, that's not a win-win-win life.

If you are a home body and do not perform at a high level in your place of passion, that's losing.

Lastly, if you are meeting quotas and growing market share, but you are not making a difference in the lives of those around you, you are missing out on a truly balanced winning life!

Balance is understanding energy and time investments in all areas of your life.

Balance is making sure you are feeding yourself, mentally and spiritually, as much as you make sure you are physically fit.

I speak to my teams all the time about the perfect offensive possession in the game of basketball. The perfect possession has all 5 guys playing at an intense pace, with outstanding spacing.

All 5 guys are playing to their strengths, whether they are a great passer or shooter or driver. There is a constant rhythm to the way they move, like a beautifully choreographed dance.

The ball has life meaning. It is moving and hopping from one player to another. But if you have all these things without balance and all the players reside at one side of the court, the defense is easily able to guard them.

Balance and understanding of where each player is in relation to who has the ball is the key ingredient to great offense. Thus creating win-win-win offensive basketball.

The same is true in all of our lives. Balance is crucial. Understanding that harmony must exist in all aspects of us personally, but also understanding that balance is needed in the professional, personal, and communal aspects of life to achieve comprehensive greatness!

Ultimately comprehensive greatness can be described with another word...happy!

# Balance

## By Virgil Herring

Balance is the foundation to life and all the situations in which we may find ourselves.

Balance is informative. When a certain outcome happens, it can tell us if we are out of balance.

When I am working with a golfer, balance is where their swing begins and ends.

That means that when a golfer begins and finishes his swing, if he is able to be in balance at those two points, not only is it easier to be in the correct positions during the dynamic parts of the swing, but incorrect positions become actually more difficult to get into.

So being balance actually makes a bad swing more difficult than a good one!

In the same way, balance in our lives – emotionally, physically, and spiritually help us to be more successful in each area and make poor decisions, emotional pain, and physical problems less likely.

It is balance that prevents us from falling and it is the pursuit of balance that helps us to rise again.

# Chapter 12

# <u>Analytics</u>

## By Drew Maddux

Analytics has changed the way our world lives, works, and plays.

The capture and understanding of advanced data elements can and will affect how consumers buy products, business leaders make decisions, investors make buying or selling decisions pertaining to business entities and stocks, and lastly, analytics has affected how we make adjustments inside and outside the game we coach and play.

Data has always been used as a truth teller of how we are performing, but with innovation and the further developing of advanced tools and technology, we can now make even better choices in our next move.

The question is how you process the enormous amount of information and apply it to your pursuit of excellence.

Yelp has affected the restaurant where you had dinner last night.

Fandango is spitting out reviews for the last movie you saw.

You look at stars for a driver before deciding what Uber to choose to take you to the airport.

The way we view athletic prospects has totally changed as we look at recruiting sites.

Companies have entire departments dedicated to advanced decision support systems to make their next move.

The way we coach has been extremely affected by the way we do video breakdown, cut ups of games, advanced reporting to develop scouting reports, and the ability to help in player development based on the information we have.

Yet the question still comes back to your philosophy. What is your culture about, and how do you penetrate those elements with the information you have to drive improvement and efficiency?

The way I coach has totally been affected as now, in game, in real time, I have staff members dedicated to looking at several statistical elements that 10 years ago I would not have even heard about.

I am wanting to know things like points per possession on the defensive and offensive end as I know we should be averaging over a point per possession of the ball and defensively should be holding our opponents to less than .90 points per possession.

I do not want to just know our traditional field goal percentage of shots made or missed. I want to know "effective field goal percentage" as that takes into account the type of shot we shoot and the value placed on that shot meaning a 3 point shot has 50% more value and therefore can adjust your effective field goal percentage.

I want to know turnovers per touch and deflections on the defensive end and to make sure we are getting 17.5

possessions per quarter. That is information I want to know real time, in a game.

Outside of the game, we are studying trends and patterns. Seeing shot locations, personalized shot selection, player tendencies, other teams' willingness to do certain things.

We have so much information that we can allow to help us in elevating the performance of our staff and our players but, as I tell people all the time, I cannot coach a game just looking at the numbers.

I cannot coach a game just viewing the scoreboard. Taking the information and allowing that into your decision making is great, but intuition and that "gut" feeling still helps the great ones be great.

Analytics, information, and data are amazing as is the way technology has made that so easy to access with our smart phones, but the human mind is still, in my opinion, the greatest collector of advanced analytics.

# Analytics

## By Virgil Herring

Analytics have changed so many sports in and over the last 10 years.

Moneyball in baseball, long distance shooting in basketball, and complete tee to hole breakdowns of golf.

Analytics don't guarantee wins, but it does show trends where games, series, and tournaments are lost and where gains can be made.

In golf, analytics can help take emotion out of the decision-making process. By having a complete understanding of shot variance, proximity to the hole, probabilities, and stokes gained/lost information, one can tailor their practice down to the essentials to consistently give them the best shot to be in contention.

That is why everyone plays the game. To have a chance to win at the end. That is when it gets fun.

# Chapter 13

# <u>Coachability</u>

## By Drew Maddux

There are "know it alls" and "learn it alls" and in order to have a chance at experiencing greatness, you must be one that is thirsty for knowledge.

Being coachable starts with humility and being receptive to learning from anyone and any experience you encounter. The day you stop striving to be around people or in situations that stretch you is the day you have zero chance to be great.

The great ones always want to learn. The greats want to be coached. The greats are looking for ways to learn new ways.

\*\*\*\*\*\*\*\*\*

A few years ago, after we won our first state championship in 2012, I arrived back on campus for the first day of school.

We had just gone 37-2 and won the state championship and we had most of our players returning the next year. I knew we would be the best team in the state of Tennessee and the expectations for this team in 2012-2013 would be extremely high. That morning I pulled my truck into my usual parking spot on our campus and the crazy thing was, I was paralyzed and could not get out my truck.

My emotions were running high and a very high sense of anxiety had taken over my innermost being.

I couldn't get out of my truck because as soon as my feet hit the pavement, I felt it would be symbolic of this being a new year. And with a new year, we would be expected to win another state championship.

I was thinking that I'm not sure I'm equipped to lead this group of boys through this again with the enormous pressure and with all that this team would have to face.

So I sought out help. I needed a coach. The coach needed a coach to help be a guide and provide counsel.

I have always thought of myself as being coachable and I realized I needed help, didn't have all the answers, and wanted someone to help coach me as I coached my team.

I called one of my closest friends and mentors, a guy who was further down the road than me and someone who had a heart aligned with the way I view the sport to help me. I called him and said, "I need a coach...can I share what I am feeling now and you help coach me through this experience?"

I told him I needed him to be a truth teller. I needed him to be a safe place and I needed to be able to have the confidence to share things I was feeling.

He agreed and we began to meet every Thursday at 8:00am. We met every week that year and still to this day view 8:00am on Thursday mornings as sacred time as he still is coaching me.

# Coachability

## By Virgil Herring

This is a very unique word for me. To be great you must have a lot of self-trust and belief in yourself and your abilities. But you also must know who to trust, because no one gets there alone.

I believe there has to be a level of understanding of where you want to go and where you are.

Allow the guidance of those who have led others down that path to success, provide conclusive evidence to how, why, where, and when it can be done. Coachability lends itself to other key words in our book such as trust, commitment, growth mindset, teammate, and love.

Coachability is a condiment of greatness because everyone needs guidance on this rocky path to success.

# Chapter 14

# **Competitiveness**

## **By Drew Maddux**

The great ones love to compete.

They love to compete against the one across from them. They love to compete against themselves in pushing to be better. They love to compete in the moment, never backing down from opposition.

When I think about competitiveness, I think about the separation from those that are average and those that are elite. I think about quality being the difference of being good or being great.

I think about Jim Collins in one of my favorite books, "Good to Great," taking 2 companies in the same industry and explaining the difference between why one company went on to be highly successful and why one company's growth stayed flat or even went backwards.

Jordan, Brady, Jobs, Gates, Manning, Tiger, Bird, Magic just to name a few, loved to compete and took great pride in figuring out ways to defeat their competition.

Within my practices, we are always putting our players in competitive situations. Shooting drills, on-on-one defensive drills, 5-5 work, regardless of what the exercise is within the framework of practice, we are always putting the players in a situation to build the habits of what it takes to compete.

Consequences are always on the line because we want to build into the situation a motivating factor to get addicted to what it takes to compete harder, longer, and with more determination than the person you are going against.

As John Wooden used to do at UCLA, we make the practice environment harder and more challenging than even a game.

I feel you are always building the traits of being an elite competitor. I believe these skills can be learned and grow over time. The more you compete and care about competing, the easier it becomes each and every time.

\*\*\*\*\*\*\*\*\*\*

Growing up I knew basketball scholarships at the Major Division 1 level are limited. Further, I figured at my dream school, Vanderbilt University, they would only sign on average 3-4 players in each class.

Last I heard, over one million players play high school basketball so the competition is massive for those limited spots.

I had to compete each day to make sure I was separating myself from the guy next door, next state, and all over the country.

Many days I would go to bed at like 10:00pm and as I was getting into bed, realize that on the West Coast, it was only 8:00pm and there could be someone still shooting or working on their game to get a leg up on me. So even if it was winter time, I would get out of bed, put on my basketball clothes, and go back outside to get in more work.

Competitiveness is a quality that everyone can control. You can be the best in the country at effort because that is between you and you alone.

# Competitiveness

## By Virgil Herring

The trait that rises to the top for the greatest of the great is competitiveness.

It extends beyond one sport or game. Those who achieved the status of being in the conversation for greatest of all time in the world of golf, such as Jack Nicklaus and Tiger Woods, enjoy competition and want to win at whatever they do.

Competitiveness is the joy of putting your abilities and years of hard work to the test against the same in someone else, but competitiveness extends beyond that to even games or tasks that you have little to no experience or history with.

The great ones I've studied had a drive to win at whatever they played or did no matter how seemingly small. It could be a game of checkers or competing in the Super Bowl and the greats seemed to have a knack to make things go their way.

Perhaps the reason that the greats aren't just competitive, but are great at being competitive, is because they compete much more than the average person who might not care if they won or lost at a game of Uno.

The greats want to win at everything they touch.

# Chapter 15

# <u>Resiliency</u>

## By Drew Maddux

To be great, you must have deep elements of resiliency.

As a human performer each and every day, regardless of who you are and how great you are at what you do, you will never attain perfection. That means that along the path of attaining and achieving, there is always going to be mistakes, failures, and losses.

Resiliency is the piece in your value system that makes you want to keep going, get back up, view everything as a lesson, not a loss, and try again.

The great John Wooden said it this way:

"If you are not making mistakes, then you are not doing anything!"

We are never going to make every shot (on the course or court)!

We are never going to win every game! We are never going to close every deal! We are never going to execute flawlessly! But resiliency keeps you believing, it keeps you coming back, it allows you to fight!

I love how Michael Jordan frames resiliency:

"I've missed over 9,000 shots in my career. I've lost almost 300 games. 26 times I've been trusted to take the game-winning shot and missed. I've failed over and over and over again in my life. And that is why I succeed."

Think about that, the greatest basketball player to have arguably ever played on this planet gave credit to making mistakes, losing, and failure as a reason to why he was driven to succeed.

When we think of Michael Jordan, we think about the shot in Cleveland, the six 3-pointers in the First Half in NBA Finals, the take off and slam dunk from the free-throw line in Chicago, or the walk-off shot in Utah, giving the Chicago Bulls their 6th championship!

You may also think about the shot, in the Superdome in New Orleans, over a stretched hand of a Georgetown defender as a freshman, giving legendary Head Coach Dean Smith and the North Carolina Tar Heels their first National Championship.

When you think of Michael Jordan, you think of SUCCESS. You think of greatness. You think, "I want to be like Mike." (Remember that old Gatorade commercial?)

Yet, when Michael Jordan was asked about success, he pointed to life's best learning moments of making mistakes, losing games, missing shots, and experiencing failure as the reason he was able to achieve.

He learned at an early age when he was a freshman at Laney High School in Wilmington, NC that being cut from the varsity team was not the point, the point was about response and not allowing that moment to define you. Your ability to respond to what just happened is directly tied to your level of resiliency!

# Resiliency

## By Virgil Herring

To be resilient is to be able to handle adversity and get back up to fight again.

Attitude is critical to resiliency. To know you gave it your all, no matter what you had that night, left it all on the course, floor, field, mat, or in the pool and either won or learned is essential in order to be the greatest version of yourself.

You will not win every game. You will not be the greatest forever, if you even are wildly fortunate enough to ascend to that title. But if you get knocked down, beaten badly, upset, shocked, embarrassed, or humiliated, the question is, can you get up off the mat?

When I think of resiliency today, I think of Tiger Woods 2019 Masters victory. Not only did he lose at golf, he lost his marriage, business partners, friends, and his health, plus struggled with an opiate painkiller addiction to boot.

He fought back against all odds to win and in that, he is a beacon of light for everyone.

He essentially struggled epically in every way possible, and did so in front of billions, to overcome it all and climb the mountain one more time to prevail. Truly amazing and a spectacle of resiliency.

70

## Chapter 16

# Grit

## By Drew Maddux

Grit is a throwback word that has made its way back into modern day qualities that employers, educators, and coaches look for in players, students, and employees.

Angela Duckworth had a lot to do with the word being used in circles today in her book entitled, "Grit," and her famous Ted Talk presentation. Grit is now even being used by educators in secondary schools' systems as something that is being measured and assessed through assignments and tests in classrooms across the country. Hiring practices now include the evaluation and references of grit to determine worthy candidates.

Grit is the ability to stick to it, push through, and rise above the task or circumstances you are in.

Grit is something I am always speaking to our players about.

I think about Pete Rose diving head first to slide into third base. Dennis Rodman being parallel diving for a loose ball. Or, Brett Favre scrambling for one extra yard in pursuing a first down to keep the drive alive. Other athletes who come to mind are Steve McNair and Brett Favre. But Grit is also applicable in entrepreneurial and scientific circles and applies to technology developers staying long after everyone has gone home to get the code written just right or scientists in a lab running test after test to see if their hypothesis is correct.

Grit keeps you on task, focused, and looking for the ultimate solution.

Over years of speaking about grit to parents and to students, I developed an acronym for grit to break down the word.

G-Greatness is upon you (the realization you were created for success and the belief you have what it takes!)

R-Relentless response-regardless of what just happened, I am going to answer the question of "now what?" and press on!

I-I can and I will! I will conquer this task and I will overcome. Positivity Is the key to Grit!

T-Trust the Struggle-mistakes, failures, and struggle will happen but, lean into those experiences and trust you are being built for something greater and being taken to the next level!

# Grit

## By Virgil Herring

When I think of grit, I think of uncompromising resolve to your love of the game. The ability to grind through unforeseen challenges, pitfalls, and pain to still deliver a high-quality performance.

Love and character are key words for grit. I believe you must love your game and vow to fight as hard as you can while honoring your character.

Some people I think of who demonstrated grit to rise above and deliver epic performances are Gary Player, Seve Ballesteros, Bobby Hurley, Ben Rothlisberger, Tim Tebow, and Kirk Gibson.

Coaches love gritty players. They dive for loose balls, they value possessions, fight for pars, and they offer no excuses.

**Chapter 17**

# Adaptability

**By Drew Maddux**

Being adaptable is such a crucial element the great ones possess. Things change. Time moves. Improvement is ever happening. Market conditions morph. The great ones are continually improving and adapting to what the situation is and what the circumstances dictate.

I think about the way offensive philosophies have changed in the NFL and the NBA and the way those coaches have had to change the way they prepare.

Big men now work on perimeter jump shots and market conditions have changed so that you must stay up with the current trends.

Fashion is always evolving and adjusting to consumer desires and adaptation is critical to have a thriving business.

If you know me, you know that ultimately the way I want to build my system with our team is fast, quick and vertical.

We want to speed the game up and play at a faster pace than our opponents.

We have led the state of Tennessee in scoring several years and our offensive efficiency would rank in the top percentile for high school teams across the country.

I believe in skill development and practice planning that makes our players totally comfortable with making the game more chaotic than our opponents are used to. Fast and furious and always on the attack. This philosophy has made us very difficult to play against and I know that if we create a certain pace, we will be successful at a high percentage.

I say all of that to build context to a story from a game in 2016. We were playing against our rival; this was a game that both school communities looked forward to all year.

Every year our teams have played, both schools have had numerous college players. Heading into this particular season, we had lost 5 players that went on to play college sports and our team did not possess the athleticism this particular year as that of our rival school.

That year they were very good and had the number 1 player in his class in the country and numerous other high-level college players. They were better than us, way better than us. I thought they were probably 15 points better than us.

So, I did what I needed to do to give our team a chance to win. I had to go against everything I believed and everything I had taught our guys and in 2 days of practice prepared our team to play at a very slow pace.

We were going to shrink the game and lower the possession count and limit the chance for our rival to have the ball. We have no shot clock in Tennessee and we could take advantage of that and play defense with our offense.

First things first, I convinced our guys this adjustment would be the best way for us to play. We prepared, we met, and we showed film and I showed them how we would space and slow the tempo down.

The players bought into the concept and strategy and we went on to upset our rival that particular year by 3 points. It was a win that I will always remember. I will always remember our community cheering as the buzzer went off and our students rushing the court to celebrate. I certainly will remember the locker room and the elation and joy.

No one will remember or care that we adapted the normal way we play. That the game may have been more "boring" compared to other ones that I had coached before.

They will, however, remember what it felt like when the buzzer went off and the bragging rights our school had for a year!

Had we not adapted the way we play; I am certain we would not have experienced victory. The great ones adapt, adjust, and change as needed to make sure they are in a position to be successful.

# Adaptability

## By Virgil Herring

Being adaptable is vital in so many things in and out of the sports world.

Being in the world of golf, I'm of the opinion that little or perhaps nothing requires more adaptability than what golf requires of its successful.

In golf, not only does the course change, but each course is subject to playing entirely differently based on the weather or based on what the weather has been like in the days leading up to the tournament.

New elements of danger such as water, bunkers, or rough come into play based on the wind, temperature, and if the turf is dry, wet, high, or low. There's even different types of turf/grasses that require different shots and correctly diagnosing those.

It's not as simple as assigning a yardage to a particular club.

What's more, golf adds another element that other sports don't in that equipment is constantly changing, evolving, improving and becoming more tailored to an individual player.

If you don't keep up with changes to equipment and how those changes could help you be more consistent, hit the ball further, be able to take a full swing to yardages that you face more often, and get more forgiveness for your specific misses, you could fall behind other players of equal or even lesser abilities.

Adaptation requires attention, knowledge, and action. It is the understanding that simply giving your best is more than continuing the status quo or working harder. Sometimes it's working smarter and finding ways to outsmart who you were yesterday.

## Chapter 18

# Persistence

## By Drew Maddux

Persistence is positive energy placed in a direction or with motivation continually over and over again.

Persistence is determination, a focus placed in a direction and not allowing yourself to turn to the left or right or be distracted.

Persistence is like your son or daughter that is relentless in pursuing that treat or that toy that they want and they will not leave you alone regardless of how many "No's" they receive.

There is a Japanese proverb that reflects an important and shared ideal: "Nana korobi ya oki" (literally: seven falls, eight getting up) means fall down seven times and get up eight.

Persistence is what gets you back up. It keeps you coming back over and over again. Persistence falls in the family of resiliency. Regardless of what just happened, get up, view it as a learning experience, and keep moving forward. Even if you should fall one thousand times, you just keep getting up and trying again.

When I think of persistence, I think of legendary Hall of Fame North Carolina State Coach Jim Valvano. Coach Valvano was a bigger than life national champion coach. He coached numerous NBA players and won what has now become the biggest underdog story in the history of NCAA tournament, beating the Houston Cougars in 1983. He was extremely successful as a coach but, his impact far exceeds just his winning percentage.

Coach Valvano contracted cancer and it was a brutal fight for his life. Months before he died, he founded the Jimmy V foundation for cancer research. At the Espy awards that year, weeks before he died, he gave an inspirational speech and, in that speech, he encouraged all of us to, "Never give up!"

Persistence is, "Never giving up!"

# Persistence

## By Virgil Herring

Persistence is essential when things don't come easy or as easy as you expected.

There are certain types of opponents/competitions that will make you keep coming back, not giving you an inch, until you finally breakthrough.

Breakthroughs come in all shapes and sizes. Some due to the appreciation of your preparation, some to your excellence, some to your grit, but yet there are some at the gate of success that for whatever reason want to see how bad you really want it.

Most people find these opponents the biggest pain. But maybe they are testing your true love for the endeavor. You can't be "the King" if you can't endure and persist.

I believe most people feel at the end of the journey that the persistence was the biggest pain and gain.

David Goggins, decorated Navy Seal AND Army Ranger is living demonstration of persistence. "Can't hurt me" is the ultimate thesis on persistence. The story of will, desire, and persistence in the book is epic.

# Chapter 19

# <u>Responsibility</u>

## By Drew Maddux

"To whom much is given, much will be required." Luke 12:48

When I think about responsibility, I think about this quote from the Bible. Responsibility is an expectation that as humans, we all grow into. We are all responsible for our own actions, thoughts, and feelings. Yes, but bigger than that, what is your ultimate responsibility here on this earth?

Responsibility is living out of the framework of thinking about others before myself. It is looking for ways to make other people's lives better because you entered the picture.

It is a commitment, a call to action, and an accountability charge all at the same time.

We are all responsible to something or someone, but the question is, are you responsible to yourself and the elevation of self or are you living a responsible life in looking for ways to advance goodness in the lives of those with whom you live, work, and play?

Coach Don Meyer was a fantastic coach at Lipscomb University and was an amazing mentor of young men. He invested in his player's lives and felt responsible to help usher boys who came into his program into manhood by the time they graduated.

He took time outside of the court to speak to his players about the expectations all human beings should have and ways to leverage their gifts for the good of others through service. He also was a brilliant camp and clinic coach as he created unique experiences for young players every summer and for young coaches looking to grow in the profession.

I had the privilege of hearing Coach Meyer speak many times growing up in basketball circles or at chapels in high school. One thing he said that had a profound impact on me and I still use when I speak to people is "Pick up the trash!"

Yes, "pick up the trash" is literal. You should look to make the environment and setting you operate in better by cleaning up, straightening up, and never passing trash without picking it up but, larger than that, Coach Meyer was speaking to a larger meaning and it is our collective human responsibility and that is to leave people, places, and things better than the way you found them!

People should feel better about themselves because of the way you loved and served them. Work environments and organizations should be more life-giving because of your attitude and effort and acceptance of this responsibility. Environments and communities should be noticeably different because of the way my gifts are used for those around me.

Responsibility is always about others, never about self. Pick up the trash. Coach Meyer would be proud!

# Responsibility

## By Virgil Herring

Responsibility is an essential fundamental in life. I am responsible to my family, my job, my teams, my friends, my followers, and my leaders.

Understanding what you are responsible for is the key. My golfers need to be responsible for their sleep, hydration, food, body language, warm ups, game plan, strategy(s), emotional management, and commitment to the process. That seems to be a lot, until you compare that to being a parent. Whew....

Fending off temptation to do something against the process is usually the first thing that goes. Cutting corners, short cuts, skipping steps and blaming others or something other than yourself for what happens.

Extreme Ownership by Jocko Willink is what comes to mind for me when I think of responsibility. How he viewed his responsibility during war was exemplary.

Never pass the buck of responsibility on to anyone else.

Own what happened and learn from it to be better tomorrow.

Pain hurts but it is also a training device.

Error is human, not failure.

Failure and struggle are ubiquitous among us. It is how we deal with it that reveals our character.

# Chapter 20

# <u>Vulnerability</u>

## By Drew Maddux

Vulnerability is the willingness to be real, the laying down of any false pretense of who you are.

Vulnerability is essential in having true relationship with people because being vulnerable means being honest and trustworthy without worry of the outcome.

So many times we live in relationship where people get just a piece of who we are, but not all of us, because we exist in that relationship still worrying about what the other person will think if they knew all of us.

Being vulnerable is the extension of my entire being to someone else with total transparency. Vulnerability is hard, very hard, especially in today's world of social media where we compare and compete and present to the world only the best version of who we are because we fear what someone would truly think about us if they knew all of us.

My entire life I have struggled with trusting people because I did not want to be vulnerable with others. I allowed people only to know a piece of me because I feared if they knew me fully, they would not like what they experienced. So, most of life I lived an arms-length away from people and not in full connection.

Until I met my wife, I probably was not 100% vulnerable with anyone, including my family I grew up with. I hid things from those who cared about me and never with full confidence shared how I was feeling which led to many days feeling very lonely.

I learned through the early days of marriage (and now 20 years later) that if our relationship was going to be life giving and beautiful, I would have to lay that down and trust that she would love me unconditionally, even if she knew my deepest darkest feelings, hurts, and pain.

I learned so much from my wife and have applied that to my most meaningful relationships now deep into adulthood. My most enduring and impactful relationships are with those who I can be completely honest with, laying down my worries and fears, and walk into being totally vulnerable with the other person. But the greatest joys are always on the other side of our greatest fears and you must step in faith and trust that your vulnerability will be handled with extreme care.

# Vulnerability
## By Virgil Herring

Being vulnerable is about preparation and willingness to improve.

It's not easy, at first, to swing a club in front of a camera and then have an expert expose swing flaws to you. But if you want to improve, you have to know what is costing you or what potentially could.

It's takes vulnerability. It's takes revealing your weaknesses and trusting that the one you are opening up to can help you.

We do that in life as well and it is a way that we can become stronger. We go to counselors in a similar way that we to coaches and consultants. We often seem more comfortable opening ourselves up to professionals than we do to those closest to us for fear that the imperfections that they see might turn them away from us.

What many people realize is that it can help you grow closer to the one you love. It's important to know that they can love you no matter what, even if they realize that you need help. To get to the other side requires being vulnerable to the right people.

## Chapter 21

# <u>Focus</u>

## By Drew Maddux

It is impossible to create, accomplish, or design anything without first a clear focus on the ultimate goal. Distraction will never allow you to get to your goal. Not being all in, will never get you to your destination.

Focus brings it all together. Focus allows the narrowing of the mind and your senses in a direction that leads you to your goal.

We are all process people, meaning we are always on a journey of becoming all we were created to be but, to be present in the process, which is a requirement, you must have precise focus.

No golf shot ever hit successfully was ever struck without a focus of a strategy and a focus on the shot process. To be successful in any venture or business opportunity, you must focus on your solution and the problem you are trying to solve.

I could always shoot the basketball really well, but in order to be great at shooting in game conditions, you must have focus in practice. Focus on the target (back of the rim) and focus on my shot process and mechanics of doing the same thing all of the time.

I love to make trick basketball shots. It's something I find joy in and something that brings joy to other people, whether they see it on video or live in person.

Some of these shots are incredibly difficult and I've even broken world records with length, height, and even blindfolded. One shot I made in 2016 was from the roof of the Omni Hotel in Nashville, TN.

I attempted to make a shot 300 feet in the air with all sorts of environmental elements effecting the shot. In order to make the shot, which was 300 feet high and 100 feet out away from the building, every inch I adjusted the shot from on top would affect 50-100 feet down on the ground. Add changing wind, the way the ball spins, and other factors, and you have the making of a very difficult goal of placing a ball in a hoop. It would be like trying to hit a hole in one with the odds stacked against you.

Media outlets were there and live news was being shot with 2 helicopters flying above me to capture the shot. With worry and distraction, I had zero chance of making the shot, so I controlled what I could control which was my focus. I would watch the shot and make adjustments high above the basket. I would adjust the ball spin and shot location and basically pick a spot a couple of feet from my face and focus to hit that spot.

I am glad to say I made the shot and it's now been seen by millions of people around the world. Focus and visualization was the key factor in meeting the goal of getting that ball in the basket. I love the saying "Be where your feet are."

Quit worrying about what just happened and quit worrying about what may happen next and focus on the present moment and win that moment through focus.

# Focus

## By Virgil Herring

It is easy to see when you are spectating. That locked in look. Nearly a gaze, an easy look of ferocity, and an I-mean-business face.

The ability to focus is a trained gift, but some have easier access to it than others.

Certain sports make it easier to get it as well. The more dangerous it is, or faster it is, forces the mind to go there - literally.

Focus is a right brain function that is completely in the moment. The past missed shot is not on the mind and the future important shot isn't either. You are totally in the now.

Many ingredients feed into focus such as love, desire, and competitiveness to name a few.

Each person has the ability to work on it and refine it, but not many take the time to do it.

Focus is like a muscle. Train for it. Elite performance is located there.

## Chapter 22

# The Process (Revisited)

## By Drew Maddux

The Process is what gets me out of bed every morning and excited to live the day.

The process is why I coach. We are in the process business of seeing boys grow into young men when they exit our program.

I have already stated that coaching a 15-18-year-old kid in today's culture is very difficult, probably no more difficult demographic to serve. There are so many distractions and the culture is pulling them in so many directions that they buy into a vision of what they feel a successful person at that age looks like. The problem is, all the things they subscribe to as success are elements of false manhood and we are trying to set up a process of manhood manufacturing where they understand they were built for others and to be in relationship and to be a part of something that is bigger than their own agenda.

We stay focused on doing the next right thing and allow the results of the scoreboard, wins and losses, made or missed shots, C's on tests, etc. take care of themselves and do not define us as human beings.

This is much easier on paper than it is in real life.

The original British definition of a "coach" was discovered in 1556 and described as a large 4-wheeled, horse drawn carriage used in transportation of someone from one place to the other.

Essentially, a coach is someone who helps people move from potential to purpose to production, essentially the process development of the person they serve.

The process hurts. The process is hard. The process will have high points and in the next moment low points, but we live with results and stay focused on the next element of the process.

I have studied many programs, organizations, and leaders for many years. I am fascinated at how people ascend to greatness and what was their person-centered process to get there.

I have studied different sales methods from organizations when I was in sales management. I have studied successful athletic teams. I have studied individuals who went on to be successful. But, in my opinion, no process is like that of becoming a Navy SEAL.

Basic SEAL training is 6 months of long, torturous training in sand, swimming in cold water in the dead of night, long runs with weighted backpacks, sleepless nights, and enduring long hours of being cold, wet, and utterly miserable.

Add to the physical elements, professionally trained officers built to make you question yourself continually and to answer the call to quit.

The process separates out the weak and elevates the toughest minded warriors who exist in our country. In this process, the Navy is also looking for future leaders who can rise up over the constant fear, hardship, and the ups and downs. It is the very toughest training and is a more hardship in 6 months than you could endure in a lifetime physically, emotionally, and mentally.

The process is what keeps you coming back and what we learn from the Navy SEALs process is that you can endure much more than you even think you can, but the challenge is not allowing the results or the good or bad to distract you from who you are becoming.

# The Process (Revisited)

## By Virgil Herring

When I revisit process, I believe the key is to understand that you need multiple processes to be successful in sport, business, and life.

The process of assessment is critical for improvement. This is a very deep dive on multiple fronts. When breaking down performance, it is not just the numbers and ax's and O's. How well did I sleep the night before? How hydrated was I for the performance? How was my nutrition going in to the event? If any of these 3 were less than stellar, this would help us understand poor decision making, poor emotional control, and poor effort.

In golf terms, when tour players assess their day they look at quality drives, approach shot proximity to the hole, up and down percentage (short game proficiency) and stroke gained/lost putting. One of the trickier stats is the up and down percentage. Usually my best players struggle with understanding that their stats are not where they want them to be because of where they hit their shot.

This usually stems from a player being aggressive trying to hit it very close to the hole on difficult pin placements and just missing the mark by the tiniest of margins. This is called "short-siding" yourself. When short shots are played from above the hole or with very little room to land the ball to get it close, it makes it hard for Phil Mickelson to get it up and down, let alone a mere mortal.

So whether it be in sport, business, or life....be sure to "fine-tooth comb" your assessments to be sure you don't waste time working on something that doesn't need work and neglect the actual problem. I am sure you can find many things in your life that at first seem obvious but after further review was a little more complicated. Try to find your best processes in each part of your life to help steer you through murky water that inevitably shows up in everyone's life. The process sets you free.

# Chapter 23

# <u>Positivity</u>

## By Drew Maddux

In December, 2012, our team was playing in a nationally prominent event called the King of the Bluegrass in Louisville, KY.

This was actually our second time to get invited to this prestigious tournament as we had won it the year before in 2011 and we were attempting to become only the 3rd school in the 40-year history of the event to win the tournament in back-to-back years.

We had a really good team that returned 4 starters from our first state championship team and came into the event undefeated and ranked for the first time in the school's history nationally in the Top 25 by MaxPreps. We were good and were the favorite to win the event, but we had a loaded bracket and it would be very difficult to win 4 games (in the state of KY) on 4 consecutive days.

In the first round we played another out of state team, Philadelphia Technical Magnet School, and won easily, although they were very good.

The way the bracket shaped up, in order to win the event we would probably play the #3, #2, and #1 ranked teams in the state of Kentucky on 3 consecutive days. For you non-basketball fans, that is as daunting a challenge as you will ever face in high school athletics.

In the quarter finals, we played Louisville Trinity and won a very ugly game by 8 points which set up a semi-final game against Bullitt County East High School, a team loaded with potential college players, including a 6'10" forward that went on to play for the University of Kentucky.

We knew this would be a very tough game, but we were up for the challenge. I remember the walk-through that day and the plan we put in place. I can remember the pre-game speech and plan delivered in the locker room and I felt our guys had a great understanding of the way we would play and I felt we were ready.

The game went the totally opposite way than I wanted it to go as the pace slowed and they made us play in way we were not comfortable with. They had all the momentum and as the buzzer sounded at the end of the 3rd quarter, we were down 15 points and everything that could go wrong, had gone wrong. We were out of sync and dealing with adversity for the first time in a very long time!

What is a coach to do? What are you supposed to say when you have 60 seconds in a huddle to re-frame the next 8 minutes? Most coaches I have had in my lifetime would have yelled and screamed and thrown a clip board or two. But I chose a different way and learned so much that night as I chose to be positive and convince them in the midst of adversity, struggle, and discomfort, they still, with a positive belief, could do the unthinkable and come back and win the game.

I passionately pleaded with them, encouraged them, and attempted to deposit as much positive energy as I could into them and made one defensive adjustment that was the last resort we had.

We came out of the huddle fired up and all the sudden it clicked We started to make plays which led to made shots. We grabbed rebounds we were not getting. We started getting deflections and steals that were uncharacteristic of their senior led team. Amazingly, we came back and won the game by 1 point and outscored the #2 team in Kentucky by 16 points in the 4th quarter, marking the largest comeback in that amount of time I have ever experienced.

So, what changed? What adjustment was made? Was there some basketball genius move that I instructed? The answer is no! The answer was in the choice to be positive and to allow that energy to splash onto the next guy and the next guy and it became contagious to the point that our guys believed they could do something remarkable.

Positivity is a choice and must be present in the process of continual believing that the next thing, next decision, or next thought could immediately change the circumstances I am in.

Positivity is the seed that leads to any movement forward. We tell our campers all the time they have a choice of 2 fictional characters. They can choose negative energy and be an Eeyore. Or, they can choose to bring positive energy like Tigger.

That night headed into the 4th quarter, our guys chose to be a Tigger and it created a memorable moment they will never forget. Let's all choose to be a Tigger every day!

# Positivity

## By Virgil Herring

Directly related to confidence and attitude, actually the equation of confidence plus attitude. Being positive sounds confident. Being positive is being optimistic in the face of adversity.

The ability to walk into a huddle on the sideline, or a conversation with your caddy, positivity is exuded and difference making when one can be reminded that no matter what has happened thus far, we have prepared for this moment all of our lives. Every now and again we need a reminder that we can change the momentum by choice.

Tony Robbins talks about changing your state. Get your body language in Superman pose, increase your heart rate with a burst of energy, and decide to be better now.

Remember, positivity is a choice based on your training. You will not rise to the level of the circumstance; you will fall to level of your training. Choose to trust your training and choose to believe the current situation allows for you to demonstrate what you have trained your whole life for.

# Chapter 24

# Confidence

**By Drew Maddux**

When I think of confidence, I think of Mike Tyson walking to the ring in his black trunks, black high tops, towel draped over his shoulders, eyes locked and loaded toward his opponent knowing with certainty the fate of the other fighter was going to end in a knockout, probably very early in the fight.

When I think of confidence, I think of Kobe Bryant entering his "Mamba mentality" state after he has made two shots in a row and knowing with certainty the defender that drew the role of trying to defend him was going to be in for a very long night because Kobe did not see the defender, he had entered a state of only a relationship between himself and the basket and nothing was going to stop him.

When I think of confidence, I think of the relationship between Joe Montana and Jerry Rice or Peyton Manning and Marvin Harrison or Tom Brady and Rob Gronkowski and the relationship of trust that was built into knowing with absolute certainty if a pass left the hand of one of these Hall-of-Fame quarterbacks, it would be caught by their favorite target because of the confidence that had been built into that relationship by hours and hours of practice time together.

When I think of confidence, I think of Jack Welch and the certainty he led General Electric when he took over as CEO. He was steadfast, strong, brilliant and had the confidence in himself and his executive team that their strategy deployment had zero chance of not succeeding.

Confidence is earned day after day after day in the unseen hours of preparation and practice.

Confidence emerges as the brain sees history repeat itself over and over and over again.

Confidence is tied to repetition as the chemicals in our brains fire off reminders of moments and events that tie our present to moments in our past of achieving that exact thing.

Confidence can be shaken and unsure if we do not prepare for the moment enough at performance and game speed.

Confidence is tied to positivity, vision, and belief as those must be present. But, if you want deposits of more confidence in what you are trying to do, clock in when no one is watching so you will be prepared in the next moment when people are present and watching.

# Confidence

## By Virgil Herring

Confidence can elevate a weak player. Lack of it can bring down an otherwise great player.

I have talked about how important being committed to your shot is in golf. In fact, I've said that it's better to be fully committed to the wrong shot than to not be committed to the right shot.

The same is true of confidence in that it's better to be confident of a less-than-perfect game plan than to be unconfident of a good game plan.

Confidence produces follow through, momentum, and focus. When doubt is in your mind, focus on your goal is nearly impossible to obtain because your mind is tossing around doubt and uncertainty.

Confidence is akin to bravery in that bravery is not the absence of fear, but acting in spite of it.

Confidence is similar in that the confident person doesn't pretend that obstacles don't exist, but the confidence of the greats is an inner belief that they can overcome and that they can deal with the adversity if they don't overcome at first, to do so eventually.

## Chapter 25

# <u>Embrace</u>

## By Drew Maddux

To embrace is to hold tightly, to grab firmly in your grip and say I accept this moment, person, or experience fully.

Embracing is saying good or bad, I am willing to face and focus on what is coming my way because I hold dear to what matters. I am locked in because I have all I need to move forward because I believe in myself and my preparation and I believe in the people who are facing this with me.

Embracing comes through preparing for the moment together and the love and connection that is strongly formed because of a shared experience and the mindset that we have what it takes to do anything.

So many times in my life I have been reminded that embracing and trusting other people, co-workers, and teammates is essential to the accomplishment of a task, game, or obstacle.

Being fully focused and locked in during the moment of competition or during an experience was so important because I fully brought my present self into it. As a leader and coach, to assemble a group of people together in a shared experience for a common purpose in a moment in time, is a very difficult task.

So, the embracing of each other's strength and weaknesses, recognizing giftings, being present in the moment and wrapping your heart and mind around the experience is so very important.

My wife and I adopted our 2 sons from Uganda. We had gone through so much in the process of trying to make this dream a reality in 2009 and 2010. We met with countless families who had walked the road and adopted before us. We prayed continually and sought council and coaching from our church and from other adoption organizations.

We worked with the government on getting passports, visas, social security cards, guardianship paperwork and that was just in the United States. We had to prepare for the Ugandan items needed governmentally as well.

Working with the orphanage the boys were living and being cared for had its own process as well. And then there was the financial side of just adopting the boys. Much less even thinking that once they were here in our house, we would be charged to care and provide for them, not just financially, but be their parents and love them in every way unconditionally.

This process required much faith and embracing the process and the call on our lives to walk this road. It was very difficult as things did not always go smoothly-papers were not returned, credit card charges ran up, government and judicial processes slowed, but we were locked in and embraced those challenges.

In October 2010, my wife and I traveled to the other side of the world to Jinja, Uganda to meet our sons. I will never forget the way I felt after 36 hours of travel by planes, bus rides, and down dirt roads.

When I stepped out of the bus on the grounds of the orphanage and my sons were placed in my arms, I embraced them as I only had 3 other times in my life when my 3 daughters were born. These were my sons and all the struggle to get to this moment was worth it and would continue to be worth it daily the rest of their lives because of the connection we had as father and sons. Being a Dad is the greatest calling on my life and that day of embracing my 2 sons is a daily reminder of the "all-in-ness" full embracement requires.

# Embrace

## By Virgil Herring

Embrace - acceptance and to hold dearly.

To embrace struggle is to understand that it is a given and is there as feedback to developing a better version of yourself.

To embrace team, as something bigger than yourself, ultimately allows everyone to fly higher. Unity of vision, one heartbeat, oneness of wholeness.

To embrace a brother/sister in the field of play/battle is to enjoy the competition and all that it brings to your life. Life is about competing, not only winning. Life is way better with a group of like-minded teammates than it is to achieve something by and large alone.

To embrace the moment is to accept what it is, not make it more or less than that, and then leave it all on the field, court, or course.

The embrace of a loved one in victory or defeat is one of the most cherished memories anyone can have. Human touch is so powerful. Embrace all that is good, even with its mysterious looks.

# Chapter 26

# <u>Passion</u>

## By Drew Maddux

Passion is what gets you out of bed in the morning. Passion is what keeps you coming back. It is a burning desire to be great, make a difference, and impact the moment.

Passion determines your "Why" and is at the epicenter of anything and everything that has ever been accomplished. You cannot press on without a passion to do so.

It elevates the higher calling of why you do what you do and the "Why" is always more important than "What" or even the "How."

Passion is love, it is on the move, and is contagious. Without passion being present in your situation, there is absolutely no way you can be as successful as you hope to be.

Passion keeps you at the gym long after everyone has gone home. Passion gets you to the office early to work a little longer on that report or presentation.

Passion is in every calling and connects us to be inspired to something greater, something larger, something better.

Passion is fulfilling regardless of monetary gain, titles being awarded, or trophies being won.

Passion is coming alive as you do what you were created to do.

I had always heard growing up that life is being lived at its maximum level when your passion becomes your paycheck. I never understood what that meant as a young professional in my early 20s coming into the work force.

I was just ending my career in basketball and a tremendous void was in my heart and soul and wrongly so as I realize now, my identity was totally wrapped in my performance.

Significance and success were defined with how I played. So I felt now that I could not play basketball anymore, what do I do next?

The answer I thought was found in making your way in the business world. That happiness would come from the success I would gain and the money I would earn with some company selling some product.

Maybe you can relate to this thought. Don't get me wrong, I worked for a great company and worked with and for some incredible people, but I looked up after 6 years working like crazy and moving up the corporate ladder and wondered if this was it. Was this what I was created to do? Does this bring fulfillment to my life and speaking life to me and my family?

The answer was no because it was not fueling my true passion and calling on my life.

The next year, as a 29-year-old, I thought maybe there is more to life than this, maybe I was created with giftings that should be leveraged in a different way, both to make a difference in people's lives, but also to wake up and have a burning passion that breathes life into what I was doing.

Basketball and service were two things that I always loved to do. I obviously had a passion for the game and I have always loved serving other people through camps, clinics, Sunday School, etc. So, I volunteered to be a middle school basketball coach in the 2005-2006 school year.

At the same time, I was reading a book my Pastor had recommended called 'Season of Life" by Jeffrey Marx. The book was about a guy named Joe Ehrman and the way he coached football at a high school in Baltimore, Maryland.

While I was coaching that year and reading that book, I became alive in a way I had never encountered. My passion for using the game of basketball to impact and connect young people in a shared experience was growing each and every day.

That year I felt something that I had never felt before and that feeling was my Passion rising up in my heart and mind in a way that created a level of joy never experienced.

After much consideration and conversation, I came to the realization that being a coach was my true calling and my true passion. In spring of 2006, I awoke to this call on my life and met with the CEO of our company and said I was going to coach high school basketball.

It was a real sense of purpose and answer to a call to action that is hard to explain and many people, including our CEO, did not understand.

I was leaving a great salary, incentives and bonuses, upside potential, and stock options to say yes to this call. Passion is what I was saying yes to and 14 years later there is not one day I regret that decision.

I have been fortunate to wake up and be a high school basketball coach and use the game I love to love the people placed in my path of life! That is passion!

# Passion

## By Virgil Herring

This is the secret ingredient. The passion for what you do is essential for greatness. It is what pushes you to new heights, it is what keeps you going when times are tough, and what you cling to when you celebrate victories.

Passion burns inside of you. It is an inferno that can't be stopped. The love you have for whatever is the sun to your being. It creates life every day. It is the oxygen, the fuel, the fire, the food - whatever it needs it gets.

Find your passion and make it your life.

My passion is to help kids achieve their dreams.

I didn't have much coaching in golf. I had to figure it out on my own. Many, many attempts fell short until I actually found what was missing.

Generally speaking, it was too late to apply it to my own game, but perfect timing to never let that happen to anyone I coached.

I have been blessed to have helped (as of June 16, 2019) 178 junior golfers get a college scholarship. Each one is as special as the next. But I have also "saved" a few excellent talents from quitting because they were on the same road as I was in 1995.

I have been honored with awards in the past, but nothing means more than the affirmation of my passion, and helping kids achieve their dreams.

## Chapter 27

# Enthusiasm
## By Drew Maddux

I love when you encounter someone who has great enthusiasm for life. Circumstances may come and go but, they have and unwavering enthusiasm regardless of the result.

Raining outside, doesn't matter. Sunny outside, doesn't matter. The result goes their way, "Great!" The result doesn't go their way, "Great, let's get better!"

Enthusiastic people are the same and environmental conditions, unpredictable circumstances, or the result they desire has no relation to their measure of enthusiasm. Enthusiastic people change the room. When they walk in, you know they are there because the positive energy dial just went to another level. I know of no one who does not love being around enthusiastic people.

When thinking of enthusiasm, I have learned so much from my 11-year-old son. He was born in Kampala, Uganda, a town of 1.5 Million people looking for hope in their lives.

Life is different in Uganda as many of the needs of life are difficult to meet and life has extreme hardships in general. I learned from their culture when I visited there that the people have a genuine joy for life and appreciate the small things as much as the big things.

My son was left by his biological mother or father as an infant for someone to find in order to better provide for him. This is a cultural problem as over 2.5 million orphans make up the population in Uganda.

A police officer found this little baby boy that was under-fed and malnourished. To say his beginning days were a struggle is an understatement. My son is a fighter, a survivor and his world was unpredictable until we met him at the age of 2. He then was taken to an orphanage to be cared for and that is where our story intersected with his story.

His eyes have seen more grief, hardship, and hopelessness in his short time on this earth than mine have seen in 40 years. But my son has joy, he has had this joy since the day he was placed in my arms. I have never seen anyone like him that leaps into the day with excitement and enthusiasm.

He loves the big things and the small things. He appreciates a trip to the grocery store just like he does to Disney World. He loves life and his enthusiasm has changed my house and my family forever.

His teachers share with us the same thought and say the classroom is different because of him. I coach him in sports and I watch the impact he has on his friends and teammates.

When I grow up, I pray I have the same enthusiasm for life as my 11-year-old son!

# Enthusiasm

## By Virgil Herring

My favorite infection is when I am with someone enthusiastic about life.

Enthusiasm is contagious. When I think of enthusiasm, I think of Tony Robbins, Arnold Palmer, and my friend Brendon Donelson. They lift up a room with their way. Every ounce of them gushes with enthusiasm.

The love of life, the love of following a passion, the love of the competition. It is effusive and magnetic and can't be faked. The energy is real and it is uplifting in times of trial, a guidepost for a challenge, and a battery charger for exhaustion.

The human body almost has no limits except what our mind creates, and when the grind, the struggle, the challenges get brutally tough, I have always been supercharged to back up off the mat because I hear Tony Robbins uplifting me with his encouragement. Every team needs one.

124

## Chapter 28

# Engaging

## By Drew Maddux

The ability to connect a message to an audience or recipient is engagement.

Engagement is two-way and requires a feeling, emotion, or message to clearly be communicated from a sender and then received by another group of people or individual.

Engagement moves forward with consistency, understanding, and agreement. The measurement of messaging and communication comes down to the way engagement is the bridge from sender to receiver. To be engaging is inspiring and moving and can be with someone you know very well, a speaker, a social media post, or being in an arena with thousands of others. Engagement inspires, creates a call to action, and moves both parties toward the best version of who they were created to be.

When I think of engaging experiences, people, and moments, my mind races to some of the best movies, greatest speakers and preachers, games I've been to, articles I've read, and lastly concerts by some of the best performers in the world. But if I close my eyes and really consider a time in my life where I felt total engagement, the kind of engagement where you don't look at your phone, care about what you have to do tomorrow, and lose every worry and anxiety, would be the Sam Hunt concert at the iconic amphitheater in Red Rocks.

I was "all in" and locked in when I stood there in this venue that has hosted the greats so, just being there up in the Rocky Mountains with the moonlight cast down and the stars shining bright was incredible in itself.

To be in that place, with full appreciation of understanding the incredible performers who had played that venue, was an amazing feeling. And, then, to be there and watch Sam Hunt deliver a performance I will never forget, had me completely and 100% engaged.

Every piece of me, mentally, emotionally, and spiritually, was fully connected to that experience and that's engagement.

When was the last time you experienced that? How was your heart and Mind opened up because of the way you were engaged in that experience? With engagement, comes personal growth and that is a quality the greats have!

# <u>Engaging</u>

## By Virgil Herring

Engaging is what I feel when I receive direct eye contact, a sense of connectivity to what I am saying/doing, and an attentiveness to the moment.

Some people have the ability to make you feel like you are the only person in the room. Arnold Palmer was that way. His eye contact and a bizarre sense of connectivity to you while you were talking with him was his amazing gift. So many people other than me feel like when he was with you, you were the only thing that mattered at that moment.

Engaging in a moment is only subtly different. Eddie Vedder, Garth Brooks, Taylor Swift, and Kenny Chesney, to name a few, are musicians that are engaging in their events. They feel connected to you and show it and feel it with you during their live shows. They draw you in extra close to them and actually share the connection with you while they perform. Not every act can do that.

Engaging in a game is to give you full attention, positive energy, and connection to your team while in the game. The best leaders usually have this engaging style about them. They grab your heart first before the grab your hand to lead you.

# Chapter 29

# <u>Risk-Taker</u>

## By Drew Maddux

To do anything worthwhile or pursue doing the unthinkable or unattainable, there has to be an element of overcoming fear and taking a risk.

There is always a moment in time where your mind says "Retreat" or "Attack" and risk-takers are always on the attack!

The great leaders, players, and executives are brilliant at taking into account calculations from many different directions and then stepping forward in a direction - that is risk-taking.

Risk-taking is moving in faith when you are not positive of the result. It's the willingness to go against the grain, swim upstream, and look foolish as you know and feel you are taking a chance.

Many great organizations or companies started in a trajectory with taking a risk. The New England Patriots hired a fired coach in Bill Belichick to lead their team years ago and that risk has paid for itself many times over. The Golden State warriors drafted a skinny little point guard from Davidson College in Steph Curry and he changed the fate of a franchise. Steve Jobs kept taking risks and testing new ideas and without his willingness to be unshaken and take the next risk, we would not have iPhones.

In order to understand risk, sometimes you need to look at history to better understand future application.

There is no better risk-taker in the history of the United States than George Washington. The culmination of breaking away from Great Britain and the official formation of the United States was July 4, 1776. At that time, The U.S. had 23,000 troops and Washington was named unanimously the Military General of the military.

To put this in context of the situation, he had never led more than 1,000 soldiers. In August, after signing the Declaration of Independence, George Washington lost the Battle of Long Island in his first major battle. That loss led to the British capturing huge territories in New York and New Jersey and forced Washington to retreat and protect Philadelphia, the capital.

The question then arose, "Should he retreat and play defense with hopes we can save what we have but realize we will never get New York and New jersey back?" Or, does he take the risk and go on the attack of the British in those territories?

To make matters worse, his numbers are depleted because of casualty numbers and others choosing to go home and leave the war. He also knows on January 1, 1777, men can leave the army because their enlistment time is over.

This set the stage of Washington attacking Trenton, NJ with 3,800 men (he had lost about 19,000 men) in December, 1776.

The British controlled many communities and towns throughout New Jersey and it was only a matter of time before they attacked Philadelphia.

On December 25, 1776 (Christmas night), Washington took 2,400 men and crosses the Delaware River through the snow.

The river was ice-packed and there were many other environmental obstacles. It would be easy for him to have said, "This is too much to overcome." When he crossed the river, he was 3 hours behind schedule and 2 other regimens were unable to cross the river. So, another decision had to be made - should he go alone or should he retreat?

He chose to attack because the risk was worth fighting for.

He divided the 2,400 men into 2 groups to make the appearance of surrounding Trenton to appear that there were more troops than there actually was. To add to the matter, he was attacking not only the British, but, he the Hessians (German hired soldiers).

When the U.S. attacked, a full-fledged battle set out. The U.S., with this surprise attack, captured 900 Hessian soldiers and forced the British to retreat. Therefore, this risk by Washington to fight to capture Trenton propelled him to another great victory at Princeton and because of those combined victories, enlistment went up, moral soared, and ultimately forced the British to retreat to New York.

These victories saved Philadelphia along with the confidence of an entire country and if he did not attack and win those battles, who knows what the United States would be like today or if it would even exist?

In learning from Washington and any great leader, you must be willing to take a risk that can lead to long term sustainability and growth. The great ones take risks sometimes and choose to play offense!

# Risk-Taker

## By Virgil Herring

Some people have an unrealistic view of their ability to be consistent. Yes, confidence and optimism are vital, but it's also vital to understand that you are an imperfect human being.

That means that the best performers among us factor in their human element when they are making decisions.

In the world of golf, that means that even the very best realize that they will not hit every shot the way that they plan. This does not shake their belief in their own greatness, it simply adds another challenge and another item for them to consider when they are developing their strategy.

Among the greats, however, is also a type of six sense or a willingness to take a calculated risk when necessary. For a golfer, that could be on the last hole when you are down by one and you choose to go for the par five in two even though there are penalty areas surrounding the green.

It could also mean that you take dead aim at a flag even though missing the green would be costly. Sometimes the risk makes sense if the reward could mean victory.

The greats know when to take a risk and do so with the understanding that risks don't always pay off. They do so with confidence, believing in themselves to pull it off, but being willing to forgive themselves if they don't.

## Chapter 30

# <u>Grateful</u>

## By Drew Maddux

I love being around people who are grateful. They have a full appreciation for life, for acts of kindness and service, and for other people and their story.

Grateful people have a way of making situations and environments better because of their attitude and approach to life.

Grateful people are humble, are selfless, and are always thinking about ways to make other people feel better.

Grateful people are great leaders and teammates because they recognize they cannot do it alone and recognize the beauty and giftings of other people. They have a way of celebrating other's success and get more excited about other people succeeding than they do themselves.

I have had the privilege of coaching some outstanding young men who have been extremely coachable and were great teammates. There are no better young men to coach than those who possess the quality of being grateful because they are hungry for teaching, coaching, and appreciate you wanting what is best for them.

One young man I think of is a young man named Jeff. He graduated a couple of years ago and he loved to play basketball. He did not possess the most natural ability, but he worked extremely hard and was an incredibly encouraging teammate.

After every practice, he would go up and shake every coaches hand and say thank you. At the end of every game, he sought out the officials and the scorekeepers and he would express appreciation. He always encouraged his teammates and was amazing during practices, games, and in the locker room. All of this started with him being grateful to experience our basketball program at that moment in his life.

On senior night, we do a special thing by tradition and have our seniors write their "Legacy Report," which is their life story (obituary) and they read it to our younger players and their families. This has become a sacred process and it is amazing hearing an 18-year-old write their vision for their life.

When Jeff, delivered his story, his story was not like any other story we had heard. I am not saying the other seniors' stories were not good - they are all beautiful, but Jeff went to another level of detail in his Legacy Report. He went through every single player (freshmen through seniors), coach, manager, trainer, and supporter, having to be at least 40 people and he thanked each person for the way they had spoken life to him and encouraged him. His deep level of grateful expression was unlike anything I had seen or heard in my lifetime.

He celebrated big things, small thing, and all moments in between and how each of those people had inspired him and pushed him to be the best he could be. It was beautiful and Jeff taught me what living life through a grateful lens truly looks like.

Great leaders are grateful for everyone's contribution. They celebrate other people's success more than their own and realize they can't do it all by themselves. Life is a big team sport and in order to experience true joy, you must have a grateful heart and live a life for others.

# Grateful

## By Virgil Herring

Grateful people have a full heart of appreciation for everything they have in the present moment. Yet the grateful among us also have an amazing ability to find something to be thankful for even during tremendous struggle.

The ability to take time every day to pose a thought of all the amazing things we have in our lives is getting lost in our society because we have generally lived in an extended period of time of no tremendous struggle. No homeland war, no rash exposure to disease, no famine, nothing for most of us that takes away the general staples that we forget are a privilege.

Great leaders speak often about being grateful for the simple things that allow them to focus on more specific endeavors that bring them joy and wholeness.

When I think of grateful, I think of how many people helped me and my family during the flood. With no power, no way out, and a flooded home and business, people came out of the woodwork to bring us food, help clear out the house after the water receded, and helped rebuild our home. It is a moment that I will never forget. It restored my belief in humans. That nearly everyone is good, and just want happiness and peace. Watching the news had mildly tainted my view of civilization.

No matter what you think the world is today, it is mainly full of people trying to do good things.

## Chapter 31

# Accountability

**By Drew Maddux**

Accountability is the bridge between immaturity and maturity. When you finally realize the comprehensive expectation of what it means to be a woman or man, you have stepped into full maturity.

Accountability is the trait that allows you to step outside of yourself and understand the full connection to a cause and that life is about relationships. In order to understand what accountability means, you have to consider others better than yourself and you must seek to elevate those around you.

Accountability is a selfless trait because you are accountable only to yourself when you remain selfish.

For over 20 years, we have hosted a basketball game at our gym at 6:00 AM every Monday, Wednesday, and Friday. 3 days a week, 52 weeks a year, for over 20 years.

With the game starting at 6:00AM, I wake up most on those days at 4:30AM to get to the gym and get stretched and loosened and to make sure my body is ready to prevent injuries. Regardless of what has happened the night before, a late night at the office, a late game, baby kept me awake at night, or it was a sleepless night, accountability to my friends and the other guys playing gets me up and to the gym. There is a group of guys that are counting on me to open the gym, unlock the doors, have the basketballs out, and turn the lights on. This is accountability.

If I only thought of myself, some of those mornings it would be easy to hit the snooze button or even turn the alarm off and say I am tired. Accountability to my responsibility of opening the gym and to the other guys gets me out of bed and excited for the day.

One of the things I do as a coach, with this thought in my mind, is I host many workouts and practices at 6:00AM in the summer or before school. The idea that I am promoting is instilling inside these guys that are 15-18 years old is that there are a group of people they are accountable to that are depending on them to be there and be present and excited to bring their best at that time of day.

Do not just be there or try to just get through the workout, but you are accountable to bring your very best because everyone is counting on you.

Accountability can be instilled, taught, and reinforced and we need more teachers, coaches, parents, and employers to hold people to a standard of accountability.

# Accountability

## By Virgil Herring

When I think of accountability, I think of Payton Manning. He not only knew his responsibilities as QB, but he also knew everyone's responsibilities on the field.

He put winning on his shoulders. He felt, as the leader of the team, that he could not actually lead them all if he didn't fully understand their duties on the field.

Accountability is the finished product of responsibility and the result. I usually find that a boy becomes a man and a girl becomes a woman when accountability is grasped and becomes part of their fabric of being.

If you want to take credit for the accolades, you also must own up to the mistakes, errors, or simply put, your best not being good enough today. That is hard to put out their because to some that means failure or not good enough. But to others it is something to use for growth.

Mindset, attitude, grit, and ownership are key words to accountability.

# Chapter 32

# <u>Transitioning</u>

## By Drew Maddux

Life is lived in moments of transition. Transition is the period of time that exists between the past, present, and future. It is the connector of what just happened and the response to what happens next. It's the moment in time that our mind, body, and soul process what just occurred and how to move on to the next play, moment, day, or period of time.

The great people I know, the great athletes I have watched and coached, and the great leaders of our generation can all process information much faster than the mediocre or average and have continual relentless responses to what is next.

The great ones have a sense of urgency and the innate ability to see things much faster than the normal person does. Think Tom Brady, Larry Bird, Warren Buffett, or Colin Powell.

Those who transition quickly have a sense of urgency and live each day like it could be their last. Seasons, days, and years go so fast as life moves in the blink of an eye. The great ones enjoy the day and have a sense of calmness as things speed up.

The way I try to get our players to play the game of basketball is to understand that every play is a two minute drill and that is how we should live our days, never taking anything for granted.

The last part of transitioning is understanding that you must finish! Win each moment, each experience, each day! That means behavior in all aspects of your life, complete immersion of yourself and the process of being excellent.

We are called to excellence in everything we do, not compartmental excellence or excellence in a certain aspect of our life, but complete and comprehensive excellence in all things.

In order to attain this level of being elite in every aspect of your life, you must understand the that life is about transitioning and how you respond to what just happened! Now what?

# Transitioning

## By Virgil Herring

In golf the transition is where most of the best players get a little off under the most pressure. We always hear: "Stay smooth in the transition" or "let it flow, not hit."

Well, when we transition in life, we are also looking for a smooth transition. Transition indicates a change has happened, or is about to happen. Things that jump out at me that help smooth out the transition are: preparation, visualization, trust, faith, and allow (not force).

I know when I was forced to transition my career either because of the flood or a management change, I clung to these principals to get me to the other side. I was prepared with my resume, work ethic, and credentials. I visualized myself being something different and better than before. I trusted that I provided value for a club or school and that I could help people enjoy this hard game. I had faith that God had not brought me this far to just drop me in my face.

That was part of my journey that I had to face. I stayed humble but confident in my ability. Humble and confident is the way. John Wooden may have said it best: "Never go into an event thinking you are superior to your opponent, but also never go into an event believing you are inferior."

Trust your process unwaveringly, and be true to it and the transition will deliver you what you need.

# Chapter 33

# <u>Power</u>

## By Drew Maddux

Power can be abused. Power is abused. Power allows people to, at times, compromise what they believe. The search and climb to a position of power can cause people to do things they promised themselves they would never do.

Power expressed correctly comes from influence gained though humble service.

The thought process of the first should be last and a servant to all. Power, if used in the correct way, gives individuals and groups confidence. It's a source of energy and a source of positivity.

Influence is the modern-day currency and power and influence should seek to be attained by thinking of others before ourrselves and the willingness to elevate everyone around you.

True power is the opposite of what you would think, it's being weak, being last, and being a servant. That is power because that is depositing a selflessness, love, care, and concern into the universe.

When I think of power, I think of people I have studied over the course of history. Dictators that used it incorrectly, or corrupt politicians or CEOs, or coaches who led and used others to self-gain. But when I personalize the word power, it becomes a positive term because one of the most influential people I have ever known was powerful and influential but did so from a posture of humility.

Ben was a special human being. He was a husband. He was a father to 5 special children. He was a theologian and historian. He was also a brilliant teacher. Over many years, he endeared himself to our school community, both parents and students, as he faithfully connected and supported everything and everyone.

Quite frankly, he was the nicest person I knew and always started every interaction wanting to know how the other person was doing. He became beloved to our students and kids sought out Latin as a course just to have him as a teacher.

A couple years ago Ben received the dreaded news of a certain type of cancer after going to the doctor and having tests run because he didn't feel well.

He fought hard. We prayed. We sent notes. We cared for him and his family but, he continued to get sicker and sicker and sicker. We received word several months later that the cancer had accelerated and he was too weak to leave his house. Because of the way our students loved him, they wanted to honor him by our entire school going to his house and singing worship songs outside his window as encouragement.

So, one fall morning, over 450 students loaded up on buses and went to his house. That incredible connection is power. While the students were there, a video was made of Ben looking out his window at the students down in his yard singing. It was an amazing sight. That video was posted and Tim McGraw and others saw it and posted it on social media and the video went viral. Viral to the toon of over 100 million people viewed the video.

Ben lost his battle with cancer, but that video has inspired millions of people around the world. His legacy lives on powerfully today as people still visit and want to attend our school because they saw the video.

That is power!

# Power

## By Virgil Herring

Power is a unique word that sounds positive until overused or abused. Power is the double-edged sword.

When I think of positive power I think of my sport and how Jack Nicklaus, Greg Norman, Tiger Woods, Rory Mcilroy, and Brooks Keopka use their power to dominate major golf events.

Power allows us to hit shorter clubs into the green which in turn gives us more opportunities to hit shots closer to the hole which leads to more birdies and easy pars.

On the other side of power is John Daly, a man so tremendously talented, but who lacks the ability to govern that power. It ultimately has been the ruin of his talent and game.

Power also reminds me off Shaq. His power was staggering. He was possibly the most overwhelming force that basketball has ever seen.

Negative use of power has occurred often in sports. I am most reminded of Albert Haynesworth stomping on a Cowboys players head in a game. Sad and terrible.

God offers gifts to us all. Each of those gifts are power. Whether it is Whitney Houston's voice, Clapton's guitar, Tyson's punch, Nolan Ryan's fastball, or Marshawn Lynch's running, each of these examples are his gifts.

Unfortunately, power has corrupted so many and in so many ways, but the real gift is to recognize the gift, practice, and strengthen it for maximum efficiency and to chase dreams along with the common good for the masses.

# Chapter 34

# <u>Sport/Work IQ</u>

## By Drew Maddux

Sport/Work IQ or, in my particular case that I will speak from, "Basketball IQ," is not like your normal measurement of a traditional IQ (Intelligence Quotient) which measures your natural, God-given intelligence.

Your Basketball IQ is yes, your intelligence in terms of the game or position, but, also your historical knowledge and the further application of those traits during competition.

When we say that a player has a high Basketball IQ, it refers to that player's thinking of the game, processing of the information, and implementation into their performance.

Players who have a high Basketball IQ make smart basketball plays that include great passes, great reactions to what the opposition presents, and the application of studied trends and tendencies.

With that as a framework for possessing a high Basketball IQ, I do believe your IQ can continue to grow, evolve, and improve and we talk to young players all the time about 4 specific things you can always do.

Even me as a coach, I apply these 4 things with a growth mindset to continue to get better and improve and shape my IQ to help the next group of players and teams I am fortunate to serve.

1. Be a student of the game

If you are a player that loves to play, you probably love to watch basketball. Not only that, you probably love to watch certain players or certain teams and may even be a fan of those teams or players. Don't just watch the game to enjoy it as a fan, but watch it as a student of the game. At my house, I keep a notebook to write down thoughts or plays I see during games. You can learn so much by just watching the game as a student rather than just a fan looking for highlights.

2. Use what is at your fingertips

There has never been any point in history that we can receive information as easy as now. The amount of great information online or though social media is incredible, so use it to your advantage and learn and grow.

3. Ask questions

Be a sponge and continue to ask questions. Ask questions of your coach, mentor, or teacher. In today's environment, many times it's perceived as weakness when people ask questions. I believe the opposite. It presents strength because you want to continue to learn and grow. The day you stop asking questions is the day you stop learning.

4. Learn from others

Many times, after a game, if another coach ran a play or executed a concept that was effective, I watch the video and try to learn what occurred. If I do not fully understand or it's not clear, then I will pick up the phone and ask them a question. Younger players should always learn from older players. But we can always have an open mind and learn from anything and anyone.

Those are 4 quick and easy things you can always do to grow in your knowledge and expertise. To attain a high IQ, you must be humble. You must ask for help. You must have a growth mindset.

# Sport/Work IQ

## By Virgil Herring

When I think of Sports IQ, I think of Wayne Gretzky and Larry Bird.

Both were excellent students of the game and had a "sixth sense" on where to be in advance.

Gretzky was noted for knowing where the puck would "be going" and be the only one there at the time, allowing him to go undeterred for a goal or assist. His scoring numbers were ridiculous, especially his assist numbers, which were another sign of IQ that recognizing sharing the goals and the limelight was better for the team and the overall attitude of dominance.

Bird was similarly amazing with his no look passes, bizarre rebounding numbers and again his ability to get everyone in the game and get their own self-belief high for the game.

The IQ piece is essential for leadership due to the ability to thrive in the intangible world. They seem to be doing mathematical equations of their sport/work on the fly and seamlessly at that.

You must be a student of the game and have a strong desire to crush the little things that become big things.

Sports/work IQ relies on passion, love, desire, and curiosity. To want to know everything for no other reason than just to be the best you can be.

## Chapter 35

# <u>Grind</u>

## By Drew Maddux

The grind is the continual process of relentless effort over and over and over again. Many times we talk about the grind being something you do not enjoy, you just endure, but the great players, people, and employees that I have studied and encountered found joy in the midst of incredibly hard work.

The word "grind" has become a word players use all over social media as it relates to workouts, training, and conditioning. The great one's mentality around hard work is different than the average and their approach and view of the "grind" separates them from everyone else.

Braxton graduated from our program in 2014 as 2-time state champion. I started coaching him as a skinny little 5th grader one spring when I started a 5th grade AAU team.

Braxton has an incredibly athletic family and if I mentioned his last name, you would instantly recognize them due to their greatness and the accomplishments. Braxton loved basketball, every aspect of it. He was a true student of the game, worked on his shooting, and did countless hours of skill work when he was younger and into his middle school years. He always was a hard worker who sought to win every sprint and competed hard in every drill. I felt his attitude towards hard work was one of "have to" rather than "want to" and was limiting how great he could ultimately be.

After his freshman year, we met in my office to discuss his off-season plan and areas to focus on in order to improve. My challenge to him was to shift his approach of how he viewed workouts and training to more of a positive mindset and seek to find happiness in the struggle and adversity. I told him he had the physical, mental, and emotional capabilities to be a Division 1 PG and to leave a legacy unlike any player before in our program.

He agreed to try that approach that off-season and it was amazing to watch his attitude toward hard work. He was encouraging of others, he was a vocal leader, and still was our hardest worker, winning every sprint and every drill. What he found was that hard work could be fun when viewed that it was changing him in every way. Braxton went on to be very accomplished, being named to all-conference teams, all state teams, and numerous all-tournament teams. After his senior year, he signed that Division 1 scholarship that he had dreamed of.

I learned so much from Braxton as he had a smile on his face and never stopped encouraging during these training sessions. He viewed the grind as he got older as a positive thing and not a negative thing. Now, he has graduated from college and received his Master's degree and is looking at what is next and I am confident that he will be extremely successful in anything he does because of his joy in the journey and the way he shakes off struggle. The grind is a good thing, you just have to see it that way.

# Grind

## By Virgil Herring

The best grinders I know are usually the ones who have the clearest picture of their goal.

That means that they have less concern for how they achieve that goal and more concern for finding a way even if their path isn't perfect.

Many people who aren't as consumed with golf as I am hear the name Tiger Woods and think of powerful drives, accurate approach shots, and drained putts. But those of us who follow the game closely know that while he certainly has his fair share of those, what has made Tiger Woods one of the greatest, if not the greatest golfer of all time is that he could win ugly.

Tiger could miss the fairway and miss the green, but still find a way to make par or better. In fact, based on the best way we have to measure today, he is the greatest ever to play at saving par.

Tiger could put his ego aside and, rather than fuming about hitting his drive behind a tree, focus on what to do in the moment to put the lowest number possible on his card.

Sure, he wasn't happy when his tee shot didn't go where he wanted it to go, but Tiger accepted that sometimes that would happen. In fact, he prepared for things to go wrong. Rather than being the most accurate ball striker, Tiger will go down in history as the best grinder to have ever lived. He found a way and narrowed his focus to the next shot instead of distracting himself by frustrations of the previous one.

In sports and in life, the greats put the past behind them and find victory in the moment in front of them. That is grinding.

# Chapter 36

# <u>Fear</u>

## By Drew Maddux

Rollercoasters, spiders, snakes, heights, and haunted houses all create a certain unexplainable fear inside of me dictated by external factors.

Failure, being alone, making a mistake, and letting someone down all create a certain type of fear driven by internal forces.

All fear is real and all fear is relative. Meaning, what scares you may not scare me and what scares me may not scare you. But when fear creeps in, it is real and can difficult to overcome.

In 2016, $8.4 Billion was spent on Halloween in the United States. That is a lot of money spent on dark and scary stuff that will be tossed out after October 31st. As a society, we like to be scared when it's controlled. For example, a scary movie or show. But we have a very difficult time as individuals processing things that make us fearful.

So why then are we talking about fear as it relates to excellence and individual performance? Great question and I am glad you asked.

When you and I came into the world as infants, we did not have fears other than basic survival fears like the need for food and water and addressing basic Maslow bottom level hierarchical needs. That means that all of those fears I mentioned about myself and all the fears you have that are created by both internal and external forces have been learned over the course of your life.

That means your fears have been taught to you and recycled in your story over and over again to the point it has become a very real fear. And as we know, anything that has been learned can be unlearned and be reversed.

In moments of performance, the greats have trained their heart and mind to unlearn the fear that may control the moment or the opposition. Fear of failing, fear of a mistake, fear of missing, fear of not trying, on and on and on, have been unlearned or are in the process of being unlearned and they have allowed faith (the opposite of fear) to occupy the real estate in the hearts and minds.

Anytime fear is present, it has control over you. Faith is what drives fear out and what leads to confidence. Confidence is what leads to overcoming. The thing to understand is that fear is tied to your future, not your past or even your present. It is not scary when you know or are positive of the outcome. In those moments of uncertainty of our future or how it will turn out, we question 2 things related to our identity:

1. Who we are - basically asking, "Do I have what it takes?"

2. What will happen to us – asking, "Will I be okay, good or bad, make or miss, win or lose?"

You and I do have what it takes and we will be ok because our identity is not a slave to performance. We must realize our uniqueness and the part we play in the bigger story and that our value is not found in success or failure. Fear controls all of us too much. It is time to allow your faith to score a knockout over it!

# Fear

## By Virgil Herring

FEAR—-False Emotions Appearing Real

Fear is energy that is mostly used to protect us from pain be it physical, mental, or emotional.

What is interesting about this is that some people use fear as rocket fuel to performance. Usually because it was a childhood response to succeed or make it through something.

I have heard so many people talk about how the fear of losing motivated them to give more effort than ever to pull through victory.

The positive lesson from this is that you can use fear to be able to create something in your mind to focus on to push your effort to the next level.

The bad news is that you can't go to that well frequently. It will not sustain. Negative energy as a positive is a limited power source.

## Chapter 37

# <u>Weakness</u>

## By Drew Maddux

The recognition of weakness is a great thing if you are being honest with yourself.

It is great because recognizing your weaknesses can be the fuel that drives you to self-improvement. But the danger of not being honest with yourself is that it will create a blind spot and you will never see the areas that need to be improved.

Further, you need truth tellers in your life that can be honest with you and tell you areas of strength and weakness. It is important that you do not get your feelings hurt from their coaching and critique.

Drake came to work out with me before his junior season at Austin Peay University in Tennessee. I was doing individual lessons and training sessions in the summer time with numerous college and professional players.

Drake was a fantastic player. He was very successful in high school, scoring over 2,000 career points as well as being named All-State. He then went to college where he experienced immediate success his first 2 years being named All-Freshmen First Team his first year and First Team All-Conference his sophomore year. He was an undersized Power Forward and heading into his junior year began to look forward to his final 2 years and beyond to professional basketball. He had an honest evaluation with himself and knew at his size he would have to improve his perimeter shooting.

Through his first 2 years of college, he had made single digit 3-point field goals and he knew he would need to transform his ability on the perimeter to evolve his game and hopefully get paid to play one day professionally. At his size, he needed to be more of a small forward with the ability to shoot to go with his strengths of driving the ball and scoring at the rim.

That summer we worked every day and shot a variety of shots to stretch his shooting abilities. We worked on mechanics, movements, footwork, and selection to ultimately grow his game further from the basket. We were consistent in our approach and followed my shooting methodology. He returned for his junior year a new player as he made over 50 3-point FGs that year alone on his way to another All-Conference selection.

We worked again between his junior and senior year to continue to refine his new reformed shooting capabilities. His senior year he made even more 3-point shots and became a career top-5 scorer in the school's history. He is now one of the premier small forwards in Europe playing over a decade in the top professional league. He credits our work in the summer of turning a weakness into a strength for his sustainability.

The recognition of weakness is a great thing in self-improvement and performance and the great ones understand that and are constantly seeking ways to improve and even turn a weakness into a strength!

# Weakness

## By Virgil Herring

The ability to recognize your weaknesses or at least be vulnerable enough to hear them from someone you trust is critical to raising your game.

I am of the belief that you can turn a weakness into a norm, but never a dominant piece. Eliminating your weaknesses are essential to growth in many levels.

When I think of weakness awareness, I think of Justin Rose. When he turned pro he missed his first 21 cuts. He was not accurate enough off the tee. Now he has turned into a solid driver off the tee. He has spent a few weeks as the #1 player in the world. That is a pretty amazing story right there.

He is not the best driver of the ball, but by just getting better at it he became the best player in the world.

# Chapter 38

# **Pain**

## By Drew Maddux

Pain to me is a great loss of something, someone, or some experience that I hold dear. There is no pain unless there is first great care or concern.

Pain hurts because of connection and investment. Pain is difficult to process because of the relationship that exists between you and the other person or experience. Someone close to me could say something that causes deep hurt and someone I do not know could say the same thing but it not even bother me.

The deeper the pain, the deeper connection. Put a different way, the level of investment will dictate the level of pain you feel. With great care and concern, there will be the opportunity to experience a high level of pain.

Pain, like weakness and failure, are also great points in our growth cycle to experience a taking off of improvement. You cannot go to the next level until you experience and master tragedy and triumph in the current level you are in.

Pain can be the loss of a loved one, loss of a job, loss of a game, loss of health. All of these could register different levels of pain on a scale, once again pointing to pain being relative (as is fear) to the person it is inflicted upon. What creates deep hurt to me may not hurt you and what hurts you may not hurt me.

Pain is that feeling of not knowing what to do next because the hurt is too much to take the next step forward. Great people I admire have had the ability to take the pain they have experienced, processed through that pain by visiting the emotions they experienced, and then utilized and leveraged that pain as they move forward.

The great ones keep moving forward even when they do not see what is next. They walk into the next level by faith, not by sight, trusting themselves and what they have experienced and trusting their closest inner circle around them to support them. They do not allow the pain to veer them off their path. They continue to stay focused on the next phase of their process and never grow discouraged. They continue to move forward.

The greats stay locked in on the present and trust they are being prepared today for what is coming next. Lastly, they realize everything happens for a reason and there is always a higher purpose and the opportunity to use the pain as an encouragement to others that may experience something similar.

Trust the struggle and lean into the pain, you are being built continually for something bigger!

# Pain

## By Virgil Herring

Pain is a sign. Pain can take an emotional, mental, or physical face.

When I think of someone who could handle pain it was Steve McNair. He was a warrior. Played with turf toe and a cracked sternum and led the Titans to victory. In my conversations with Coach Heimerdinger he would tell me how tough that guy was. How he could block out pain in his mind. Endure it like no one he had ever seen.

When I think of emotional pain I think of Brett Favre, (who actually could fit the above example too) the Monday night game he played after his dad died. It was other worldly how he played that night. Sometimes pain allows us to ignore technique just to make it. Which happens to deliver us into the zone or even deeper into flow (the mental state in which a person performing an activity is fully immersed in a feeling of energized focus, full involvement, and enjoyment in the process of the activity).

When I think of mental pain I think of Katerina Witt. As one of the most famous figure skaters ever, she was followed and spied on by the East Germans so that she would not defect from the country during and or after the Olympics.

To know that you were essentially trapped in a situation that was unfortunate and trying while still getting to do something you loved was a true sign of her mental endurance. She was given freedom IF SHE WON the gold medal for the 3rd time. To know that going in must have been grueling. I tip my cap to that.

Playing in pain and playing hurt are two different things. I never want my players to play hurt. But playing through pain is what all the greats do. Use it as fuel for greatness or allow less expectations to deliver epic performances. Know the difference to make a difference.

# Chapter 39

# <u>Failure</u>

## By Drew Maddux

Failure and the fear of it paralyzes so many of us. For most of my life, my fear of failure was a paralyzing force. I allowed a miss, loss, or defeat to bother me so badly. That carried into my professional career as I could not deal with losing the account, sale, or client, once again allowing failure and the fear of it control me.

Over the last decade through being involved again in the game of basketball through coaching, I began to work through and process why failure bothered me so much. I realized it was not so much the failure (although I hate to lose), but it was the shot to my identity and value that made it hurt so much.

So, in coaching kids and learning how to better deal with disappointment, I helped my players work through areas of loss and defeat. I ask questions like, "What are you worried?" "What is the worst thing that could happen?" You could miss. You could lose. You could be shot down. You could make a mistake. You could make a bad grade. You could not get the promotion. None of those outcomes could ever define who you are and what you are being created to be!

The seed to greatness lies in the first step out of your comfort zone and being willing to take a risk and being okay with making a mistake. Nothing great was ever decided, accomplished, created, or changed inside of a comfort zone. The first step to be great is to stare fear of failure in the face and say, "Not today!"

My identity is not tied to my performance or the outcome or any single event. I am so much bigger than that! I am so much more than that! I have so much more to offer than that!

How many interviews have you heard at halftime of big NFL football games or NCAA March Madness Basketball Games or the Pre-game show to any game you have ever watched quote, "The Team that makes the least number of mistakes will win this game!" I cannot stand when I hear coaches or announcers say that because, basically, what you are saying is that the team is going to play from the paradigm of fear of failure and not be free in their approach.

Having heard that in locker rooms my whole life as a player, as well as having heard well-respected coaches say that on television, I promised myself that if I ever coached a team or led a business, I was going to encourage my players or co-workers to attack that moment with freedom and not fear of failure.

# Failure

## By Virgil Herring

Failure is a crossroad word. What I mean by that is that when a person experiences failure in an event, they are met at the crossroads of using it as a learning tool or using it as a crippling crutch for excuses, negative attitudes and poor body language.

The sooner we can get into a place of, "We either win or we learn" rather than a "winner or a loser," mindset, the better we will get at handling the pain of losing/failing at something that we put so much time and energy into.

Golfers are a special group in this world because generally speaking 156 professionals will be playing each week and only one person will be deemed "The Winner." Here is where mental toughness training, process orientation, routines, and analytics create a recipe for a growth mindset, which will allow each person to do excellent self-analysis work. It is this, "Cycle of Champions" process that allows players to mark progress and deficiencies that will allow for proper and accurate assessment of their efforts, giving a clear gameplay on what needs to be addressed in the process to continue to grow.

One of my favorite examples of this is when, after the 2000 Open Championship, David Duval had just lost to Tiger Woods, and was in the press room taking questions from the media. He was asked if he choked coming down the stretch and what did he feel like he would need to do to breakthrough to win his first major. David's reply was forceful and powerful. "I don't appreciate you the media trying to paint me in as a loser here. I played as well as I could play. I followed my processes each shot over these four days of competition, and for that I won. I can't do any better than that. It just so happens that Tiger Woods scored better than me this week. That does make him the winner, but that does not make me a loser or a failure!"

David then used what he had learned that week to come back to the 2001 Open Championship and win his first Major as a Professional Golfer. At the crossroads of failure David Duval demonstrated a growth mindset and took the road to "I either win or I learn." That is how we should attack life and sport. Failure is a critical component to winning. It is how we learn.

# Chapter 40

# <u>Destiny</u>

## By Drew Maddux

Destiny is the process of stepping forward into your uniquely designed purpose and assignment.

Destiny is doing what you were created to do. Destiny is your passion and purpose intersected. Destiny is an uncertain future and vision, but aligning your present to that calling.

Teams and organizations can be set apart by destiny for the specific fulfillment of encouraging a fan base, customer, or other people. We hear the term all the time, this is a "team of destiny" meaning they have done things the right way, accomplished at a high level, and received some good fortune along the way. We hear the term destiny spoken in individual sports like golf when Tiger Woods just won this past year's Masters.

Destiny is connected to your ability, calling, and giftings and the fulfillment of your destiny is the recognition that you need other people to help you in the pursuit of that calling.

What you are able to accomplish, achieve, and influence begins with the determination of what is your passion and purpose and what and who you will be connected to in order to get there.

Each of us have been given a specific assignment that only we can do. Our story matters and we have been created for a specific purpose at this point in history, so what will you do to make a difference in the larger story being played out. You and I must realize that this assignment is vital and important and not get caught up in the comparison and competition of whether our role is more or less important of anyone else.

All of us are equipped or are in the process of being equipped in order to continue in the process of moving forward to our created destiny.

My challenge and charge to each of you that will read this entry is to think through, meditate on, and do some soul searching on exactly what our passion and purpose is and to ask ourselves how the discovery of those can be leveraged into advancing goodness in our communities where we live, work, and play. How do we leave places better? How do we leave people better? How are situations better because my specific gifts and my passions entered the picture for that moment in time?

Please realize that your assignment is divinely important and you must step into that calling with authority and confidence and use those gifts for the advancement of others.

# Destiny

## By Virgil Herring

What you achieve when you follow the process toward the best version of yourself while chasing the elusive visions of your dreams.

The journey is more prized than the destination. So cliché but so true. I am not sure I believe that your destiny is completely pre-ordained, but I believe the there is a strange guiding hand taking you there when you follow the process.

What is your destiny?

I feel like one of the most powerful statements I ever read was by Kevin Elko: "The two most powerful days of your life are the day you were born and the day you find out why!"

Those are some thinking words right there. Mine was 11/13/1973 and 7/26/1995 when I found out that it was way more enjoyable helping others achieve their dreams than it was for me to win a golf event. My dad was a coach and I guess coaching is in my blood. But that is the day in Chicago that I saw the joy of a player get better, win, and find out they would play college golf. The tears of joy and shared accomplishment with a young golfer never ever get old. Each one just as important as the last. I don't regret that decision at all. I have had quite a journey thus far. Whatever destiny holds for me I hope it has hundreds of teary-eyed joyful smiles with me.

# Chapter 41

# **Forgiveness**

## **By Drew Maddux**

The great people, coaches, employees that I have been around and with were amazing in their approach and pursuit of achievement.

They had a drive, were inspired, and possessed so many qualities that helped them be a great leader, coach, or performer. These people were amazing to be around and had an energy about them that was contagious to others.

They also had great intuition and great observance of situations, dynamics, and the general atmosphere of the team, group, or organization. In saying that, they also knew in their pursuit of success if they had failed others within their care in a certain way.

Maybe they were demonstrative in their actions, maybe they said something that was damaging, or maybe they just missed it in the moment with a bad play call, substitution, or read of the situation. In those moments, they are confident enough and care deeply enough to come back around and admit wrong doing and ask those in their care for forgiveness of missing it in the moment.

I have blown it so many times as a coach and it has always been my approach that when we win and have success, the players deserve the credit. And, if we lose or suffer disappointment, it is my job as the leader, to accept responsibility. I feel coaches in our culture get too much of the blame and too much of the credit, but I do believe the coach should be accountable to his team, community, fans, and publicly to the media if there is a loss or if something happens that causes defeat.

I can tell a coach is immature and identity driven when I see a press conference and he blames the loss on their players and does not take accountability. I am always quick to accept blame to my team and to others when we do not perform as well as we should. Maybe we did not prepare like we should have. Maybe we did not execute like we should have. Maybe we did not make adjustments like we should have. All being the role of the leader and coach. When those things occur, it is my job to not only accept it, but also to ask my team and those I serve for their forgiveness.

Two years ago, we were in a big conference game on the road with a team we were tied for first place with. This was a huge game as we were attempting to win our 8th straight conference title. The players felt it and I probably was a little more on edge than normal. The game started and it was one of those games that was low scoring and a close margin the entire game. Both teams were well coached and disciplined and had great players who were very familiar with each other.

We were fortunate to take the lead heading into the last minute and the other team would have to start fouling us. All we had to do was make free-throws and we would win. They fouled us with about a minute left and we were up 7. Our best player went to the free throw line and missed. They came down and hit a 3-point shot. Up 4, we inbounded the ball and they fouled again, the same player. He went to the free throw line and missed again. They came down and made another 3-point shot. We are now up 1 with 15 seconds left. They called Timeout and our players came to the huddle where I looked in the young man's face and screamed, "Make a free throw!"

I feel terrible even writing this as I am still remorseful for this. It was not like he was trying to miss it and we still had to finish this game and now I have taken away probably all his confidence.

We draw up the play to get the ball in bounds and know they will foul again. We break the huddle and go out and inbound the ball and with 11 seconds left, the same young man was fouled. He went to the line and missed the free throw again. With both teams out of timeouts, the other team came down and luckily missed the shot and we grabbed the rebound and won by 1 point.

After the game we shook hands and headed to the locker room. Everyone was excited except for me and that young man. He looked defeated and it broke my heart that I had added to the way he felt. We got to the locker room and at that point all I did was ask for forgiveness from that young man and the rest of our team. I said I blew it and I was so sorry for my words and actions. And I was praying that they would be able to forgive their old coach.

The next day I asked the young man to my office and asked for his forgiveness as well again just me and him with us looking each other in the eyes. I still feel horrible to this day.

The great ones have a great sense for the feelings and emotions of those around them. There is a human side to their greatness and having the confidence, care, and concern for others to ask for forgiveness is an incredible quality.

# Forgiveness

## By Virgil Herring

When I think of forgiveness, I only think of my mom. My mom is generally one of the happiest and content people I know because she forgives everyone's actions towards her or negatively affecting her. It is actually humbling to listen to her describe why her forgiveness of the offender is so important for her. She certainly lets the pain hurt, but let's it go due to understanding that the offender is hurting so much more.

Forgiveness is a gift for yourself, not the offender. I wish I were better at this but I am aware that I carry a few extra emotional pounds on me due to holding on to things that were done to me on purpose to negatively impact my life, career, or friendships.

But it is a fundamental of existence to be able to forgive. Most, but not all, things that hurt us are coming from a place of pain from another.

Empathy is a good ingredient to forgiveness. It is always on my mind to take all of these things into consideration before I respond to the situation. I really try to take the other person's environment into consideration before I react. Like I said not all things are done like that, but when they are, I apply a level of empathy to it and forgive them for the transgression. When I have applied that to my life I have definitely felt better in my heart and soul and I was the better for it.

# Chapter 42

# <u>Loyalty</u>

## By Drew Maddux

Loyalty seems to be a thing of the past. It seems that loyalty gets thrown out the window in the life of free-agency.

Divorce rates are up. Job turnover is on the rise. In athletics, transfer rates at the college level are at all-time highs.

At the professional level, especially in the sport of basketball, society is more interested in summer free agency stories than they are with seeing the actual team perform.

Gone are the days when people stayed at the same corporation or organization their entire professional careers.

Most of my family members were with their same organization my entire upbringing. It seems we have shorter attention spans and as soon as we cannot get what we need from a situation, we eject ourselves from it, and look for a bigger and better place.

Loyalty is something I certainly admire and appreciate. Loyalty is a trait I am looking for when I hire someone for a position within our organization. Loyalty is a two-way relationship. Both the giver and receiver of loyalty must be life-giving and it must be an experience where needs are being met.

We are an organization that is dependent on customer loyalty. Our business model is built on making sure our customers are happy and having a great experience and decide to opt in the next year and pay for private school education.

Tuition dollars of our families drive our business model and our budget is met primarily through the retention of our customers. It is our job as a school to make sure we are doing everything possible, going above and beyond what is needed, to make sure it is a joy-filled experience so that they decide the next year that our school is where they want their children to go. A great customer relationship creates loyalty.

In studying great corporations that have become a fixture of our generation, at the centerpiece of the story is the loyalty they have created. I think about Gatorade and the way they created a "I want to be like Mike" (Jordan) generation with teenagers and young adults. The iPhone took off after creation and at the time Apple invaded the market with this product, the Blackberry phone had a majority of market share. But Apple had served millions of people over many years with its ease of use, customer friendly products and that loyalty to the brand allowed them to take over the Smartphone industry and push Blackberry to the side.

I think about Chick-Fil-A and the way they have changed the fast food world. They essentially changed the fast-casual dining experience and delivered a consistent customer experience and reliable product to create loyalty and now have invaded the Top 5 world-wide rankings in revenue for the restaurant sector.

Loyalty is a relationship that is created through reliable, consistent, and caring interaction for one another.

# Loyalty

## By Virgil Herring

Loyalty to what?

It is critical to learn to find fundamentals, rules, and disciplines to be loyal to, that is for sure.

Loyalty is a dedicated mindset and determination to a person, business, or way of life. Something that you would not turn on, backstab, overthrow, or undermine even when you are no longer even in relationship with them or it.

When I think of lack of loyalty I think of Hank Haney's book, "The Big Miss" where he gave us an inside view of Tiger Woods, and not just a helicopter view, his experience and opinion of what Tiger did while they worked together and through the scandal with his wife, hiatus work with Navy Seals, and his personal life decisions.

I am sure that he was only trying to write a compelling book about the greatest athlete of our time, which he very well did, but also might have had a little revenge in mind for how he was treated. It was one of the best books I have ever read, but it was a total violation of confidentiality - especially with a figure like Tiger Woods.

When I think of loyalty, I think of John Wooden, Dean Smith, Coach K, Joe Paterno, and Chris Berman. All of these people stayed with an institution for an extremely long time, turned down more money and maybe more fame to build something they agreed to build from the beginning.

What is fascinating is that we confuse loyalty as company vs employee, team vs player, personality vs. network. Be loyal to principals, fundamentals, and your family. Not money, power, ego, or position.

# Chapter 43

# <u>Self-Control</u>

## By Drew Maddux

Self-control is a hard one for all of us. We come into this world wanting what we want when we want it.

When we are infants and as we move to be toddlers, we are demanding when it's time to eat or if we want to play with a toy at that very moment. As we move into attending school, we learn that your eyes must stay on your paper even if you do not know the answer. Your hands must be kept to yourself at all times as it's not normal to touch the person in front of you in line. There is a schedule and the teacher is in-charge so you must remain quiet when the teacher is speaking. As you move into athletics as you get older, people actually cheer against you and they may say things that are not very nice. Entire crowds will yell and scream and hope you do not do well.

With every bone in your body, you want to scream back but, self-control keeps your mouth shut. When I think of self-control, I think of Michael Jordan gliding through the air defying gravity with complete control of his body.

I think about the way RA Dickey throws a knuckleball with complete command and control over the ball.

I think about Roger Federer roaming the baseline and making sure his body is in position to return a hard-hit ball.

Lastly, when I think of self-control, I think of the restraint required when you go on the road in the SEC to play a conference rival.

When I was playing basketball at Vanderbilt, SEC basketball was at an all-time high. National championships, top 25 rankings, and NCAA bids were being led by SEC teams.

When we went to play on the road at Florida, Tennessee, or Kentucky, the fan bases were loud and vocal and quite frankly, obnoxious. But one fan in particular pushed the limits of self-control.

When we played in Athens against the University of Georgia, we would come out for pre-game shooting to stretch and loosen. Hours before the game, the band of Georgia would already be in attendance warming up. They were positioned by the basket where we came out to shoot.

For my entire career, there was one member of their band, he played the tuba, that rode me and walked the baseline and heckled me. He knew things about me, a lot about me. He knew my family, my girlfriend's name, places I grew up. He had done his homework and was relentless in being vocal to me.

It took everything in me to maintain self-control and not say anything back or do what I wanted to do which was punch him in the face. He cussed at me, made fun of me, shouted on every shot. It was terrible and I hated to go there because he was in my head. I tried to block him out but it was tough. I never said anything to him as my limits were tested of what level self-control I had, but it was hard.

The greats have self-control in all situations. Calm, cool, and collected or at least they will make you believe they are. "Fake it until you make it!" "Act as if!"

# Self-Control

## By Virgil Herring

The physical and mental manifestation of this talent is critical.

When I think of physical self control I think of Dr J, Michael Jordan, Lynn Swann, and Roger Federer. They were able to maintain centeredness while gliding through the air or diving/sliding across the court. The amount of strength in the core and also practicing the gift they were given to own the talent is part of what set them apart.

When I think of mental self-control, I think of Gandhi and Hakeem Olajuwon. Both sacrificed for something they believed in by not eating. Gandhi for political purposes and Olajuwon for religious purposes. For the sake of sport, Hakeem fasted for Ramadan in the middle of the NBA season. No matter how it affected his play, it would not deter him from his faith. No amount of pressure from the owners, teammates, fans, or the media could shake him.

Self-control on the mental side is a challenge because you have a part of your body desiring to stop the pain and another part that receives input from chemicals produced by the body or taken by the person that creates feelings that people often want to re-experience. Self-control is critical here as many fall under the pressure of these chemicals and make poor decisions that cost their team, family or business.

# Poise

## By Virgil Herring

When I think of poise, I think of Brooks Koepka right now. That dude has composure and a level of professional dignity that is off the charts. It seems if he was pre-wired for this moment. Calm in the storm, centered in the chaos, and ready to strike with without fear.

Being prepared physically, mentally, and emotionally is critical to poise. I am sure that there may be a little percentage that may be hard wired into someone, but with the correct training, one can develop poise.

The problem is that what you need to do to train for it is different and not many people like to be different and exposed. Put yourself into very uncomfortable situations as frequently as possible so that whatever environment taxes your comfort zones and triggers bad thoughts and fear gets farther and farther from the norm.

Most of the best performances start in the brain, visualizing success, preparing for struggle, and pushing for harsh environments to really make it easier to perform under duress while trying to achieve a life goal.

## Chapter 45

# Happiness

**By Drew Maddux**

Joy-filled and life giving. The great ones know and understand that they were created for greatness. They are great because they are unique and needed. They accept who they are and fully embrace the way they were made. No need to compare and compete against anyone else, just be the best you that you can be.

The greats never stop the pursuit of becoming a truer and better version of who they were created to be. They breathe; therefore, they are, therefore they are satisfied, and with satisfaction comes increasing happiness. They are created great and true happiness is fulfilled by leveraging all that you are as you extend goodness into every area of your life.

Happiness is essential in those that perform at high levels because so much of living life and performing at a high level starts with a positive mentality. Positivity and a life-giving environment are the foundation to anything worthwhile being achieved or accomplished.

Any organization or team I have been a part of that achieved at a high level had a culture built on happiness. Everyone appreciated what each other brought to the table. There was a flow, an ease of doing life, and a celebration of each other's gifts.

One study that I reference often when I discuss high performing teams and the direct tie to a culture that truly loves each other and is happy for one another was when the Dallas Mavericks beat the Miami Heat in 2011 for the World Championship.

The Wall Street Journal did a study that year of the NBA Finals to measure team chemistry. The study centered on trying to quantify how much the players care for one another. The Miami Heat that season had signed LeBron James as he joined Chris Bosh and Dwayne Wade to form what was supposed to be an unstoppable force. The force that could not be beaten though was the way the Mavericks cared for each other. In the finals, the Mavericks, led by Tyson Chandler and Dirk Nowitzki, had double the number of slaps, hugs, taps or bumps. Further, the Mavericks were 82% more likely to high five each other than the Heat.

Success is not always correlated to happiness but, I do believe the great individuals, teams, and organizations are already ahead of the competition with happiness as a part of their culture.

# Happiness

## By Virgil Herring

When I think of happiness as it pertains to competing, I think of Ronaldinho and Magic Johnson. Both play the game with a smile on their face and a creative joy in their heart. That happiness was infectious for every team they played for.

Ronaldinho was my all time favorite soccer player. It seemed like he dribbled with his feet like Magic Johnson did with his hands. In my opinion he had more skills, speed, and shots than anyone ever. But what stood out more than anything was his smile.

But when it comes to smiles and happiness to play, Magic is the king. I might say the first billion-dollar smile. He had so much fun on the court with "Showtime" that it spilled over into everyone's game. I even think Kareem smiled more and that was tough.

Happiness doesn't arise only from joy and victory. It arises from struggle and the grind and that love of the game that fills their heart up and comes out in a joyful play that elevates everyone.

Don't chase happiness expecting to only be happy, chase it for the love of your game and what kind of contagion it is for your team.

# Chapter 46

# <u>Legacy</u>

## By Drew Maddux

Legacy is living with the end in mind and aligning your steps daily to it. Legacy is what will be left behind after you are gone. You will have your family legacy passed on to your children and grandchildren and great grandchildren.

You have a legacy professionally as you answer the question, "Did I leave the company/organization better?" and "What values, habits, and traditions have been passed on to those that are still there?"

You have a legacy in the community. "Did I advance good into the community where I live, work, and play and is the world better?"

Living with your legacy in mind is living a full life, one that someone will stand up at your celebration of life and speak to. Ultimately, what matters in terms of a legacy is, what difference did you make in the lives of others (relationships) and is the world better because you squeezed every gift you had to make the world better (A Cause bigger than yourself)?

I speak to our team and our 15-18 boys all the time about legacy. I want them to understand that decisions they are making today as teenagers will have an impact to the vision they have for their lives.

We speak about false manhood and that, at an early age, our belief about our self is found in idols. Whether it is performance on a ballfield or court, what girl I date, or what my social or professional status is, all of these things are a narrow view on legacy.

We speak about issues that make you come alive and ways that you can hook your individual story to the bigger story of time and the impact you can have.

Legacy is something we invest a lot of time in. We place as much emphasis on talking about concepts of legacy as we do a back door cut, or running a play correctly.

The culminating event is our season end celebration in March of our team. We are not like most programs in that we do not give an award that night. We celebrate and honor the seniors, shower them with gifts, honor them and pray for them, and have each of them write their obituary, called a Legacy Report.

In this, they cast a vision of their life and begin to zero in on their destiny and what their life will be dedicated to. It is a beautiful articulation of vision and gets them to think about their future families, work, service, church, etc. It is powerful and effective and one of my favorite events every year.

Legacy is tied to destiny, vision, and gifting. It also centers around relationships and a cause which is true manhood or womanhood!

# Legacy

## By Virgil Herring

Your legacy grows on you. When you are a dreamer kid, you are just busting your tail trying to chase down a dream. As you get older and your dreams start to come together, you really dig into the process and do a deep dive to be as great as you can be.

The process of this can go on for a while, then one day something hits you. "What am I doing all of this for? Why all the grinding, up late and wake up early, missing small events to make it big....for what?"

To me it is about that time that I shifted to thinking about what I am going to leave behind when I am done, not what I am going to do next. I think that when we have a family, it is generally normal to want to leave your kids with a better life than you had. Leaving a legacy is not about money only. It is about leaving behind a way of life, foundations of life, principals of healthy happiness, and fundamentals of existence that allow you to overcome the inevitable struggles that will come.

Leaving that behind is as valuable as gold. Your legacy is what you build making your life, not making a living. That building is made from the pillars of fundamentals, principals, foundations, and beliefs. Choose them well and leave behind a treasure.

## Chapter 47

# <u>Consistency</u>

## By Drew Maddux

Doing something over and over and over again is consistency. You can have great habits or you can have bad habits, but either way, you have developed a go-to pattern of behavior known as consistency.

Every day the great ones wake up and determine how they can connect to who they are becoming.

"What consistent way of doing life in the choices I make, the things I say, what I listen to, and what I practice is tied to the future self I hope to be?"

Consistency is about repetition. Consistency is about forming habits and Malcom Gladwell said in his book, "Outliers," that it takes doing something over 10,000 times before it becomes a new consistent habit.

I had the privilege of coaching John Jenkins from Hendersonville, TN when he was in high school. John is an incredible young man that has an amazing support system in his family.

John is the very best shot maker I have ever seen and I have been around amazing shooters. He has the ability to make all types of shots; 3-point shots, long range shots, closely defended shots, shots off the dribble, difficult finishes with taller players guarding him, literally any type of shot. He went on to become a 2-time Tennessee Mr.

Basketball selection, Gatorade Tennessee player of the year after averaging 42.3 points per game his senior year, and signed to play at Vanderbilt University.

He entered the NBA draft in 2012, after his junior season, and was selected 23rd in the 1st round by the Atlanta Hawks (he now plays for the New York Knicks).

The accolades, awards, and statistics are incredible and point to a phenomenal ability to consistently perform when it matters most in competition. He was amazing and could score the ball in a way I had never seen a high schooler score with trick defenses, double teams, and people talking trash to him in every gym he went to.

But his story that people do not know, nor do they see, is the tireless consistent effort he gives in the gym every single day. His consistency tied to percentages is directly tied to his consistency of work ethic. The way he practices, the repetition he gets, the long hours of difficult workouts on days when all you want to do is sit down has led him to become who he is today. I do believe he was born with the gift of natural eyes and a soft touch, but he developed into who he is by the way he works day after day after day!

Consistent practice at performance speed will lead to consistent success when it matters most.

# Consistency

## By Virgil Herring

In golf consistency is the most confused word of them all. "All I want is to be consistent."

Well, what does that mean? If you are trying to hit shots that consistently go straight and long, that is not possible. But what is possible is the consistency of your process.

The genius of consistency is to never have the outcome in mind, just the process required to give you the best chance. The brain does not access the stored talent with concrete images, it does it through abstract images.

What I am always looking for is process consistency. How well do you visualize what you want, how well do you rehearse what you visualize, and how well you commit to the visualization and rehearsal?

Nothing guarantees consistent results, but a consistent process gives you the best chance for the best version of you to show up time in and time out. That is consistency.

# Chapter 48

# <u>Consequences</u>

## By Drew Maddux

There are natural consequences and there are consequences enforced by accountability to a team or cause greater than yourself.

Natural consequences are things that happen as a result of decisions you make. For example, as simple as it is, if you stayed out late, naturally you will be tired the next morning when it is time to wake up and go to work. Or, if you consistently show up late for work every single day, your employer will have to let you go.

If you do not exercise, watch what you eat, and take care of yourself, you will increasingly become unhealthy and put yourself in alignment with potential issues as you get older.

There are also consequences of accountability, meaning you have agreed to a standard and a code of conduct to be a part of a team or organization and you clearly have been articulated the boundaries of what is expected of you. When you break one of the standards or one of the rules, there is a consequence. For example, one of our rules in our program is if you receive a technical foul for unsportsmanlike conduct inside of a game, you will have to do some running in the next practice and will be subject to missing game time the next game.

There is also a combination of natural and accountable consequences when you are a part of a team. The intersection of these two in our program is cultural norms. Cultural norms speak to behaviors, choices, and habits a player has agreed to and if one of those is broken not only, will you as the individual have consequences but, the entire team does as well.

Show up late for a practice, our entire team is going to run a sprint together for each minute you are late. In one of my first years at CPA, we had a young man show up 32 minutes late for a 6:00 AM practice and when he walked into the gym, we stopped, got everyone on the line and we ran 32 sprints together. The point was made because, we have not had to run for a player being late in over a decade.

If you are about greatness, you do not mind consequences. You do not mind boundaries, standards, and expectations because you know you will give your best regardless.

When God created Adam, he even gave him expectations and consequences even though everything at that time was in perfect harmony. God said where he could go in the garden and that he should not eat from a certain tree. But if Adam did go outside of the expectations, there would be consequences which led to the fall of man. When Adam and Eve ate the fruit from one the tree God had instructed him not to eat from, those consequences occurred. Consequences are a part of our DNA and inside our wiring. They help keep us inside the lines as we chase greatness.

# Consequences

## By Virgil Herring

Consequences are opportunity costs. For every decision you make there are consequences. Some more painful than the other of course.

Consequences also equal feedback. When I mis-hit a golf shot, the consequence of the outcome also gives me the solution to the problem. It is very important to get feedback from your best efforts, and not so best efforts. Great talent + half-hearted effort = disappointment. Great talent + lack of preparation = a much steeper hill to climb. Great talent + taking it for granted = underachievement.

All of these outcomes are consequences. They also may produce victory or defeat, but definitely will provide feedback for the future. Will you take the, "I am so good I don't need to prepare" mindset, or will you take the, "That was nearly a massive setback, I need to get back on process so that doesn't happen ever again."

Not every instance provides you a chance to rectify the situation. But usually your processes have seriously broken down to find a distinct end to your road. Process process process.

# Chapter 49

# Challenge

## By Drew Maddux

You either rise up or you give in when a challenge presents itself. There is no in-between when it comes to a challenge. You either overcome or you get run over, but challenge is an absolute thing in this world.

The greats choose to meet every obstacle placed in their way and rise up to defeat it, create a solution, or outlast the competition. It is a mindset. It is a way of being. This is a view of how you see the world. I choose to speak to my team about never losing, always learning in every moment, situation, or game. We never lose, we just learn and get better to fight the next challenge that will come your way.

Life is not always going to go smoothly. There will be roadblocks and speedbumps and you must view those challenges as something to overcome or you are defeated before you began.

I will never forget my first semester as a freshman at Vanderbilt as a student-athlete. I learned more about myself and what comfort zones I could shatter by the challenges that came my way. I moved into my dorm in August. We had the weekend to get acclimated and then that Monday, life as a collegiate student-athlete was going to begin. I had been strength and conditioning training all summer and had taken some classes, so I felt like I was ready for the challenge. I knew most of teammates and had been to orientation and spent a great deal of time with my other freshmen classmates as well. I really thought there is no way it can be as bad as the upperclassmen had described, but I was wrong. Very wrong!

That Monday morning we had our very first 6:00 AM workout and oh my goodness, I can still remember the misery I felt that day on the track.

We got done around 7:30 and I had 30 minutes to get a shower and get across campus for my very first college class. I had 3 classes that morning and then had to be back at 1:00pm for my first individual skills workout in the gym. I then had to be back in class at 3:00 and then back at 4:30pm for our strength training. We had dinner after and then the freshmen had 2 hours of mandatory study hall. This proceeded for the rest of the semester. Between workouts, classes, skills training, study halls, my own study time, and also life away from home living in a dorm, I thought on that Monday night there is no way I can do this every day. But I was wrong. Very wrong.

It pushed me in ways I needed to be pushed and grew me out of comfort zones that need to be shattered. I grew up in those 5 months as quickly as any time in my life. That foundation helped prepare me for the many challenges I have continued to face as an employee, husband, father, and leader.

Challenges will come. Challenges will be met. The way you view the challenge will either allow you to rise up or give in. The choice is yours.

# Challenge

## By Virgil Herring

When I think of challenge, I think what it means to challenge as a coach and what it means to be challenged as an athlete.

Challenge in coaching is a unique activity for me now that I am a team coach. Each day, each week, and each season I need to create a vision of the end goal and then set steps, markers, and processes so that the team keeps the vision in mind as the season moves along.

But I also need to find moments that occur to challenge the team that help force a new level of focus and ultimately a new level performance. Knowing that I will not ever be able to raise my players more than 20% past their best, it is still a huge amount of improvement in a single event.

One of my favorite things to do in practice is to not let my team hit a tee shot, but move them into a difficult position, maybe behind a tree, in a bunker, high grass, or any other challenging position and make them play from there to the hole and if they make a double bogey they have to run the next hole, triple bogey they have to carry another players bag the next hole. That will get a golfer's attention. Do that for 9 holes a couple times a year and it is amazing what happens, especially when it comes to decision making.

As an athlete I was a player that needed to be challenged to push me to work harder. As much as I hated it, I needed the coach in my can to bring out the best in me. I thrived in situations that forced me to prove something. I love that impetus in life. It creates a powerful state in my body called the, "watch this" mentality. It gets me out of my head and puts me in an optimum performance state.

It is all about knowing your players to extract that greatness and demonstrate that there are no limits to how far you can go. Just the limits you set for yourself.

# Chapter 50

# <u>Provoke</u>

## By Drew Maddux

I love the word provoke. At first glance, when I think of provoke, I think of my sons in the back seat of the car picking at one of my daughters to provoke a reaction.

I think of children in a classroom where their behavior provokes reactions from another student.

I think of Dennis Rodman and the way he played the game of basketball and the way he provoked the other team and other fans to create such anger and hate towards him. He was very intentional in doing this as he wanted to mentally throw off the other players and not allow them to perform at their highest level.

But when talking about what it means to provoke, as it relates to the greats, we are not talking about picking on one another, but we are speaking to the way they are always on the attack, always aggressive in their pursuit of what they have set their mind to do.

In 2011-2012, when we won our first state championship, we led the state of Tennessee in scoring. The thought for our offensive philosophy was pretty simple - we wanted to always be on the attack. We wanted to provoke reactions from our opponent's defense through our actions. If it was a miss and we rebounded the ball, we wanted to run in transition. If we created a turnover or got a steal, we wanted to run. If the other team scored, we wanted to inbound the ball as quickly as possible, and run. It did not matter who grabbed the ball to throw it in and it did not matter what player received the ball. It did not matter what players ran their lanes to the corner or which player ran to the rim. All players were interchangeable and learned every position. We were playing position-less basketball before that was a term.

The thought was that we would constantly and relentlessly be provoking reactions which led to mistakes, which would lead to scoring for us.

We created a fun style of basketball that kids loved to play in and that led to us going 37-2, winning a state championship, and leading the state in scoring. This style and brand of basketball was not something new as North Carolina, Golden State, and others were known for this type of offense. But the efficiency and success we had at the high school level playing that was something that was new.

Our philosophy was built on pace, space, action/reaction, and leverage creation which led to bad mistakes by the defense and great shots and early offense for our offense.

# Provoke

## By Virgil Herring

I love this word! I love to provoke thought. I love to provoke action. I love to provoke positive energy from negative outcomes.

I enjoy coming out of left field with a thought, an observation, or a challenge. I understand that the dictionary offers mostly negative tones to provoke, but I choose to operate from a positive.

I coach two brothers who couldn't be more different. Yin and Yang we will call them. Yin is the oldest and is person who has a mouth that out performs his golf. Just an insecurity manifesting itself as bravado.

One day Yin comes in talking about how good he is going to hit it today in practice. He talks about how good he is and how many people stopped to watch him hit balls over the past few weeks.

He starts off that day triple bogey, double bogey, and walks to the third tee talking about how he is going to crush this tee ball 50 by me. I respond, "Hey Yin, why don't you stop talking about your game and let your clubs and score talk for themselves?

"All this blabber is just you hoping that it will impact your opponent, but it is so false confidence it is sad."

I like players who are outwardly humble and inwardly full of swagger, not vice versa.

Brother Yang is captain Half-Empty/Partly Cloudy and he makes Lou Holtz seem like boastful with all of his self-deprecating self-talk. Truly a talented player whose self image is far below his actual potential. So I say, "Yo Yang, why don't you wake up tomorrow and have a nice glass of whatever Yin drinks for breakfast so you can talk like your brother about your game"?

It cracks me up to see these two play together. So now Yin plays with a, I-would- be-humbled-and-grateful-dear-golf-gods-if-you-would-allow-me-a-chance-to-enjoy-this-shot-that-I-am-going-to-hit (wherever) attitude.

Yang on the other hand says, "Hey Coach, watch this." Now they both are playing better because their self-image is right for them to perform. Neither of them enjoyed being provoked about their self-image. But the challenge to prove me wrong has ultimately proved me right.

Now they laugh about it as they both signed great scholarships to the same Division 1 school. Sometimes I need to be Oprah and sometimes I need to be Dr Phil.

**About Drew Maddux**

Drew Maddux has been the Head Coach at Christ Presbyterian Academy (CPA) in Nashville since 2006 with a record of 371-86 (81%). While coaching at CPA, he has seen 2 State Championships (2012, 2013), 9 District Champions, 7 Region Champions, a cumulative team 3.2 GPA over tenure, 20+ players receiving athletic scholarships, 1 NBA First Round Draft Pick and multiple Coach of the Year honors from The Tennessean and Nashville City Paper.

Drew Maddux is a native of Tennessee and presently resides with his wife, Tara, and daughters, Emma, Ava, and Sarah James and sons, Patrick and Nicholas in Nashville, Tennessee. Mr. Maddux graduated from Vanderbilt University in 1998, where he received a Bachelor of Science degree in Human and Organizational Development.

While at Vanderbilt, Maddux was a four-year starter for the Commodore basketball team. During his career, Maddux received several individual awards for his performance both on and off the court. Some of the noteworthy honors he received included, ALL-SEC Freshman, USA Olympic Festival Team, First Team ALL-SEC, and Honorable Mention ALL-AMERICA honors. Maddux was also an Academic ALL-SEC member as well as being recognized as one of the Outstanding Young Men of America in 1998.

## About Virgil Herring

Virgil Herring is Director of Golf at the acclaimed Ensworth Golf Performance Center. He is a Charter Member Golf Channel Academy Lead Instructor.

Virgil was named 2015 TN PGA Section Teacher of the Year. He received the 2003 Tennessee Section PGA Teacher of the Year Award and was named 2002, 2003, 2005, 2006 and 2015 Middle TN Chapter PGA Teacher of the Year. Virgil was named a U.S. Kids Golf Top 50 Instructor by U.S. Kids Golf and named a 2015 Top 25 Elite Junior Coach by Future Champions Golf in addition to being a Master Teacher for Future Collegean's Golf since 2015.

Virgil worked with PGA Tour player Brandt Snedeker from 2000-2007 and Tour players Harry Taylor, Brad Fabel, Cliff Kresge, Vance Veazey, Garrett Willis, Bob Wolcott, Kim Williams and Megan Grehan. He has helped over 150 junior players get college scholarships. In Nashville, hear Virgil 7-8 a.m. Saturday on 104.5 The Zone.